*Puritans
Against the
Wilderness*

*Connecticut
History to 1763*

i

Author's Preface

It is a distinct privilege to have this opportunity to write about early Connecticut and its background for all those who find colonial history of interest. Inevitably, this study owes much to my earlier book, *Connecticut,* published by Random House in 1961. In the fourteen years since its publication a number of significant new books, articles and dissertations on Connecticut topics have appeared. These works have proven useful at many points, especially in the last three chapters.

As always the staffs of the Connecticut State Library and The Connecticut Historical Society have been most helpful. Special thanks must go to Robert Wilkerson and James Mottershead of the Pequot Press who have been unfailingly generous in their assistance. The Editorial Board has always provided wise counsel and shown admirable patience on problems both large and small. Mrs. Charlotte B. Ritchie was unfailingly prompt and efficient in performing the laborious task of typing the preliminary and final drafts of the text. Finally, I owe a special debt to my wife, Wilda, for her devoted and skilled efforts in reviewing the text and making substantial improvements in style and content.

Albert E. Van Dusen
Storrs, Connecticut

Spring 1975

Puritans
Against the
Wilderness

Connecticut
History to 1763

Albert E. Van Dusen

A Publication of
The Center for
Connecticut Studies
of Eastern Connecticut State College

This Series in Connecticut History
has been made possible through
the generous cooperation of

Bridgeport, Connecticut

Published by
The Pequot Press

Chester, Connecticut

Albert E. Van Dusen (Ph.D., University of Pennsylvania) is a Professor of History at The University of Connecticut in Storrs and is the Connecticut State Historian. He has authored *Connecticut* (1961), is the Editor of the forthcoming Jonathan Trumbull Papers, and is a former President of the Association for the Study of Connecticut History.

ISBN: 87106-128-7
Library of Congress Catalog Card Number: 73-83257
Manufactured in the United States of America
All Rights Reserved

FIRST PRINTING

Table of Contents

Author's Preface   ii

Editors' Preface   vi

Selected Important Dates in Connecticut
History, 1614-1763   viii

I   Backgrounds in England and Massachusetts   1

II   The Land and Its Original Inhabitants   13

III   The Pioneer White Settlers of Connecticut   24

IV   A New Charter and Resulting Boundary
Disputes   49

V   Relations with Indians and Andros   64

VI   Connecticut Fights in Four Intercolonial
Wars—1690-1763   73

VII   Earning a Living   81

VIII   Society of Colonial Connecticut   92

IX   The Puritan Becomes a Yankee   110

Documents   128

Index   137

Editors' Preface

Albert Van Dusen's *Puritans Against the Wilderness* provides an introductory survey of Connecticut life and development in the period between the seventeenth-century founding of the colony and the conclusion of the French and Indian War. Among the topics given attention are Thomas Hooker and the "liberal" River Colony; John Davenport and the "conservative" New Haven Colony; influences of geography and geology; white-Indian relations; the pattern of everyday life; Connecticut's role in the intercolonial wars; John Winthrop, Jr., and the Charter of 1662; and the Great Awakening. The volume devotes particular attention to the deep changes involved as the Connecticut Puritan of the seventeenth century evolved into the Connecticut Yankee of the mid-eighteenth century. Professor Van Dusen finds that beneath the apparently smooth facade of Connecticut politics and religion in the so-called "Land of Steady Habits" much dissent and some intense conflict existed. Nevertheless, the volume concludes that while internal conflict often cut deep, Connecticut in 1763 was a reasonably contented deferential society.

Albert Van Dusen's study is the first volume in the five-volume "Series in Connecticut History" published by the Center for Connecticut Studies of Eastern Connecticut State College and the Pequot Press. The Center for Connecticut Studies was established in 1970 to foster an appreciation of the historical and contemporary nature of Connecticut society. Housed in Eastern's J. Eugene Smith Library, the Center is collecting a variety of Connecticut materials which are being made available to students, educators, and interested lay persons through formal courses and annual workshops. The "Series in Connecticut History" does not seek to present a comprehensive or encyclopedic record of the state's development. However, it is the expectation of the Center that these volumes by providing narrative accounts of the principal forces and events in each period of Connecticut history as well as selections of primary material will bring alive to the reader the rich heritage of Connecticut's past.

A great many persons have been responsible for the preparation and publication of these volumes. Charles R. Webb, Robert K.

Wickware, and J. Parker Huber, the president, former dean of academic affairs, and director of research, respectively, of Eastern Connecticut State College, have aided the project by a number of undramatic but crucial contributions. The Eastern Connecticut State College Foundation has been generous in its support of the Series. Francis Sullivan and Robert Clapp of the Eastern Connecticut State College Audio-Visual Department have made available their expertise in the preparation of illustrative material.

Thompson R. Harlow and his staff at The Connecticut Historical Society have graciously made available the Society's facilities and resources to both the authors and the editors. Janet Nelligan, Dorothy Hulme, and Donna Baker have typed the manuscripts. The authors of these volumes—Ruth Andersen, Herbert Janick, Freeman Meyer, David Roth, Janice Trecker, and Albert Van Dusen—brought to the project not only their individual talents, but, as importantly, an unfailing cooperativeness without which the Series could not have been undertaken or completed. And finally, it is a pleasure to acknowledge the generous assistance of the Board of Directors of the Metropolitan Bank and Trust Company of Bridgeport, Connecticut.

Louis C. Addazio
Professor of History
Central Connecticut State College

Howard T. Oedel
Professor of History
Southern Connecticut State College

Harriett I. Patterson
Professor Emeritus of Education
Eastern Connecticut State College

David M. Roth, Director
The Center for Connecticut Studies
Eastern Connecticut State College

Arthur E. Soderlind
Social Studies Consultant
Bureau of Elementary and Secondary Education
Connecticut State Department of Education

Spring 1975

Selected Important Dates in Connecticut History, 1614-1763

1614   Adriaen Block, representing the Dutch, sailed up the Connecticut River.

1632   Edward Winslow of Plymouth explored lower Connecticut River for fur trading and colonization possibilities.

1633   The Dutch erected a fort, the House of (Good) Hope, on the future site of Hartford.

1633   John Oldham and others explored and traded along the Connecticut River. Plymouth Colony sent William Holmes to found a trading post at Windsor.

1634   Wethersfield founded by people from Massachusetts.

1635   Fort erected at Saybrook by Lion Gardiner.

1635   Group from Dorchester, Massachusetts, joined Windsor.

1636   Thomas Hooker and company journeyed from Newtown (Cambridge), Massachusetts to found Hartford.

1637   Pequot War. Captain John Mason led colonists to decisive victory.

1638   New Haven Colony established by Davenport and Eaton.

1639   Fundamental Orders of Connecticut adopted by Hartford, Wethersfield and Windsor; John Haynes chosen first governor.

1643   Connecticut joined Massachusetts Bay, Plymouth and New Haven to form the New England Confederation.

1646   New London founded by John Winthrop, Jr.

1650   Comprehensive code of laws drawn up, probably by Roger Ludlow, and adopted by legislature.

1660   Hopkins Grammar School founded at New Haven.

1662   John Winthrop, Jr., obtained a royal charter for Connecticut from King Charles II.

1665   Union of Connecticut and New Haven colonies completed.

1675-76   Connecticut participated in King Philip's War, which was fought in Massachusetts and Rhode Island.

1687   Edmund Andros assumed rule over Connecticut; Charter Oak episode supposedly occurred.

1689   Connecticut resumed government under Charter of 1662.

1701   Collegiate School authorized by General Assembly; New Haven made joint capital with Hartford.

1705   First Baptist Church established at Groton.

1708   Saybrook Platform, providing more centralized control of Established (Congregational) Church, approved by General Assembly.

1709   First printing press established by Thomas Short in New London; first printing of paper money (resulting from expenses in Queen Anne's War).

1717   Collegiate School moved to New Haven; called Yale from 1718.

1724   Services begun in first Anglican Church at Stratford.

1730's   Iron industry launched in Salisbury area.

1740   Manufacture of tinware begun at Berlin by Edward and William Pattison.

1741-42 Height of religious "Great Awakening."

1745   Connecticut troops under Roger Wolcott helped to capture Louisbourg.

1752-58 Spanish ship case and lengthy litigation over it.

1754   Eleazar Wheelock opened an Indian school at Lebanon (Columbia).

1755   *Connecticut Gazette* of New Haven, Connecticut's first newspaper, printed by James Parker.

1755-62 Many Connecticut troops participated in the Seven Years' War (French and Indian War).

1756   First census of Connecticut—126,976 Whites, 3,019 Negroes, 617 Indians—total 130,612.

1758   Connecticut's second newspaper, the *New-London Summary*, launched.

1763   Treaty of Paris ended Seven Years' War.

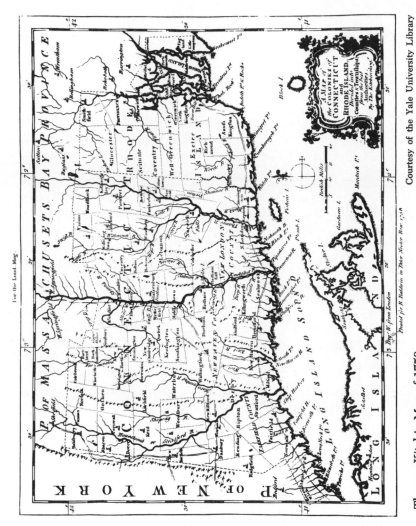

Thomas Kitchin Map of 1758.

Courtesy of the Yale University Library

I Backgrounds in England and Massachusetts

About the beginning of June [1636], Mr. Hooker, Mr. Stone, and about a hundred men, women and children, took their departure from Cambridge, and travelled more than a hundred miles, through a hideous and trackless wilderness, to Hartford. They had no guide but their compass; made their way over mountains, through swamps, thickets, and rivers, which were not passable but with great difficulty. They had no cover but the heavens, nor any lodgings but those which simple nature afforded them. They drove with them a hundred and sixty head of cattle, and by the way, subsisted on the milk of their cows. Mrs. Hooker was borne through the wilderness upon a litter. The people generally carried their packs, arms, and some utensils. They were nearly a fortnight on their journey.*

This was a short journey—approximately 100 miles—made by a small group of mostly obscure people. Who could have imagined that an important colony would develop from their efforts and those of like-minded men?

To understand how and why this little band traveled to the bank of the Connecticut River in 1636 one must make another much longer journey backward in time and about 3,000 miles across the Atlantic to England. There one will find the background and explanation for this great adventure in colonization.

England Comes of Age as a Nation

Undoubtedly the most important single fact about the first settlers of Connecticut was that they were Englishmen. Born and

---

*Benjamin Trumbull, *A Complete History of Connecticut* . . . (New London, 1898) I, 43.

bred in England, they loved their native land and left it with great regret.

Around 1500 England came of age as a nation. Cut off from the Continent by the English Channel, the English people slowly developed a distinctive language and culture. Only after the culmination of the sanguinary Wars of the Roses, however, was England able to attain some genuine national unity. Under the efficient but often brutal rule of Henry VII (1485-1509) and of his son, Henry VIII (1509-47), a high degree of law and order was achieved. The two Henrys crushed internal opposition and nurtured the growth of a vigorous nationalism and an expanding economy.

The Channel, however, offered no real insulation against powerful intellectual and religious currents which were sweeping northern Europe soon after 1500. Among these developments the Reformation proved to be the most earth-shaking in its implications.

Conditions in England were very favorable to a revolt against the Roman Catholic Church. Much anticlerical and antipapal feeling existed and Henry VIII deliberately employed this sentiment to achieve certain personal ends. Henry's marital problems served as the catalyst for a series of Parliamentary acts which carried England out of the Catholic Church and into a new Church of England with the King as its head. In form of government, ritual and most of the creed the new Anglican Church appeared very much like the Catholic Church.

After a temporary return to Catholicism under Henry VIII's daughter, Queen Mary (1553-58), Elizabeth I (1558-1603) presided over restoration of the conservative Protestantism of the Church of England. As a monarch Elizabeth inherited a striking rapport with the masses from her father, and an instinctive sympathy with their aspirations and prejudices. While one cannot credit her with creating the glories of her reign, she provided a climate conducive to their realization.

For colonization to become a reality England had to develop a strong nation at home. Under Elizabeth this was achieved. Earlier England had been too weak to follow up exploring expeditions, such as that of John Cabot in 1497, with any actual colonization.

The possibilities for future English colonization were greatly expanded by the shift in principal trade routes from the Mediter-

2

ranean to the Atlantic. While the Italian city states faced decline, the Atlantic powers—Spain, Portugal, France, Holland and England —found world-wide commercial and colonial opportunities of awesome dimensions opening to them. Spain and France loomed as England's most formidable rivals. England's defeat of the Spanish Armada in 1588 sharply reduced Spain's threat. Luckily for England, France became increasingly involved in land expansion on the Continent and largely eschewed the aggressive overseas push which might have paid great dividends.

Cabot's voyage provided England with a claim to northern sections of North America, including Connecticut. For many decades, however, England limited its American interests to fishing and lucrative raids on the Spanish treasure ships bringing the gold and silver of Mexico and Peru to Spain. Meanwhile English explorers, like Martin Frobisher and John Davis, searched in vain for a northwest passage to the wealth of the East. Overshadowing these colorful events was a solid build-up of English trade in the Baltic, Mediterranean and Orient. Private businessmen obtained charters for companies, each exploiting the trade of a specific area. After 1600 joint-stock companies entered foreign trade with marked success. Through such enterprises England slowly accumulated substantial capital—some of which became available from private investors for possible establishment of colonies.

At home slow changes spread over a couple of centuries produced a new political and economic system. Feudalism with all of its complex interrelationships and its serfs tied to the land gradually but inexorably declined. New classes of sturdy land-owning yeomen, tenant farmers and day laborers appeared as very important forces. The powerful central government replaced the feudal lord as the focus of power.

Meanwhile, the burgeoning wealth of Europe's urban centers produced a growing demand for consumer goods, especially woolen cloth. Fortunately England's climate and soil were well adapted to sheep raising. For this activity to prosper, however, it was vital to consolidate and enclose thousands of small plots of land into larger areas. Thus, for several centuries the enclosure movement became extremely important. For many yeomen, tenants and agricultural laborers the enclosures brought deep personal tragedy.

3

Driven from their land they drifted away—discouraged if not hopeless. Eventually many found work in the growing cities.

The woolen cloth industry developed into England's most profitable source of foreign income. The cloth was produced using the "domestic" system under which the capitalist "put out" the raw materials (wool, especially) into the homes of people for manufacture into finished materials. English cloth became the great staple of export to the Continent.

The cloth industry became particularly well developed in eastern England. Counties such as Essex, Suffolk and Norfolk found a new prosperity reflected in the imposing new churches seen in places like Norwich, Ipswich, Hingham and Lavenham. The arrival of skilled Flemish weavers further strengthened the industry.

While farming, sheep raising and clothmaking dominated the economic scene in eastern England, the economy was remarkably diversified for that period. Shipbuilding, cheese-making, potash making and fishing kept large numbers busy. The small port towns such as Colchester, Harwich, Ipswich and Maldon actively traded with the Continent and developed a vigorous maritime tradition. This broad economic background would provide valuable skills for the challenge of pioneering in New England, and from these eastern counties would come an unusually high proportion of Connecticut's first settlers.

Englishmen of the seventeenth century were generally accustomed to a large amount of governmental regulation of their economic activities. The prevailing economic philosophy, known as *mercantilism,* aimed primarily at economic self-sufficiency. It called for extensive regulation of imports and exports hopefully to attain a favorable trade balance. Industry at home was encouraged and chartered companies abroad helped to improve the balance of trade by selling the surplus home manufactures. Colonies played an important role in the overall plan by providing cheap raw materials and purchasing the mother country's manufactures. The mercantilists advocated a large merchant marine to secure the profits of the carrying trade.

Why in a relatively stable and prosperous nation such as England did a sizable group of citizens suddenly decide to leave to start a new life under exceedingly difficult conditions? The moti-

4

vation had to be very powerful. Central to any explanation of this migration is an understanding of the religious developments in England from the mid-1500's to the 1630's.

Under Queen Elizabeth I Parliament effected a religious compromise known as the Elizabethan Settlement. Essentially, it re-established the Anglican Church created under Henry VIII. The creed was enunciated in the thirty-nine articles passed by Parliament in 1571. Realizing that only a moderate, conciliatory, religious position could avoid intense religious conflict and preserve internal peace in her country, Elizabeth followed a religious *via media*. Naturally, a compromise church pleased neither the Catholics on one side nor the more radical Protestants on the other. Many of the latter group had sought safety abroad during the persecutions of Mary in the 1550's. Now they eagerly returned to Elizabethan England ready to implement their liberal religious views. These were the Protestant dissenters, many of whom later became embroiled with the government and church in serious disputes.

The Rise of the Puritans

By the 1560's the Puritans emerged as a separate group and grew steadily in numbers and influence. Gradually, they contained three distinct groups: (1) the Presbyterians, who followed Calvin's teachings on church government; (2) the Brownists or Separatists, later known as Congregationalists, who espoused independence in policies for every individual church; and (3) the Puritans or reformers, who remained within the Church of England, desirous of reforming it. To all Puritans the cornerstone of their religion was the experience of *conversion* which set them apart and conferred upon them the special virtues and responsibilities of the elect. This conversion might result from various kinds of experiences —a stirring sermon being a most likely one. In the process of conversion a person experienced the wrath and redemptive love of God. Puritans subscribed to ideals of strict piety in everyday living and sought to create a godly nation. Their every action was moral and required a specific accounting.

By the 1570's and 1580's they were winning many supporters by their demands that the Church of England undergo a thorough reformation. One demand which particularly antagonized the

5

Queen was that ministers, elders and all other officials be popularly elected by congregations and synods. This meant a direct reduction in the Queen's powers. In 1583 the monarch effected the elevation of Whitgift to the Archbishopric of Canterbury. He instituted very repressive measures against the more influential Puritans. In turn, they retaliated with an illuminating survey of the clergy in the Church of England. They uncovered a shocking number who fell into such categories as "gamester," "pot companion," "drunkard and ale house haunter," "unable to preach" and "incontinent." In Essex a study of 335 benefices showed 173 ignorant and unpreaching ministers, 61 pluralists, 10 nonresidents of a single benefice and 12 "preachers of scandalous life." Little wonder that Essex experienced the highest level of nonconformity in England! Opposition to the Church also reached high levels in such counties as Cambridge, Norfolk, Suffolk, Lincoln, Northampton, Oxford, Rutland and Kent. The pressure of Elizabeth's government on the Puritans was so intense, however, that the movement lost ground in the late sixteenth century.

When James I of Scotland mounted the throne of England in 1603, the Puritans expected more sympathetic treatment. Instead they found all demands for reform of the Church of England flatly rejected. Some three hundred Puritan clergy lost their positions in the Church while others conformed outwardly but worked with heavy hearts. Some could not endure the very restrictive conservative controls and emigrated to Holland. In 1620 a small body of Separatists made their famous voyage to Plymouth, Massachusetts.

For those ardent Puritans who remained in England the general situation steadily deteriorated after the accession of Charles I in 1625. He flaunted the traditional liberties of Englishmen and degraded the role of Parliament in the government to a shocking degree. By the late 1620's a depression in the wool industry added to the woes of many Puritans. Some began to consider the possibility of starting over again in the New World.

Thomas Hooker's Early Career

Among the prominent and unhappy Puritan leaders was Thomas Hooker, the future "father of Connecticut." Little is known about Hooker's parents except that they apparently possessed mod-

Courtesy of Hartford Electric Light Company. Photo by Dowd, Wyllie and Olson

Thomas Hooker (1583-1646) as he is supposed to have appeared.

erate means—enough to send him to a grammar school at Market Bosworth, a small market town in central England, located about twenty-five miles west of Marefield, his birthplace. In his famous sketch of Hooker's life Cotton Mather declared that Hooker's parents were "neither unable, nor unwilling to bestow upon him a liberal education; whereto the early and lively sparkles of wit observed in him, did very much encourage them."

These "lively sparkles of wit" carried young Hooker into Cambridge University in 1604. Most of his brilliant career there was spent in Emmanuel College where he completed the B.A. in 1608 and the M.A. in 1611. By coincidence Hooker had chosen the one truly Puritan college at Cambridge.

Earlier in the college's history Queen Elizabeth, disturbed by a rumor that Emmanuel was pro-Puritan, spoke to Sir Walter Mildmay, the founder. "Sir Walter, I hear you have erected a puritan foundation." "No, madam" Mildmay replied, "far be it from me to countenance any thing contrary to your established laws, but I have set an acorn, which when it becomes an oak, God alone knows what will be the fruit thereof." Neither Mildmay nor the Queen could foresee that one of the fruits would be the leader of the Puritan colony of Connecticut!

While at Emmanuel Hooker's entire life was changed by a lengthy, profound and agonizing religious experience. Out of this came a conversion and a decision to enter the ministry. His final years at Emmanuel—1611 to 1618—were spent in theological studies and in developing his own philosophical and religious beliefs. The works of the writer, Alexander Richardson, helped provide a basis for Hooker's thinking, but even more influential was William Ames, teacher, friend and inspiration. Hooker once said that "If *a scholar* was but well studied in Dr. *Ames* his *Medulla Theologiae,* and *Casus Conscientiae,* so as to understand them thoroughly, they would make him (supposing him versed in the scriptures,) a *good divine,* though he had no more books in the world."

A Puritan Ministry in Difficult Times

Hooker began his pastorate humbly as rector of St. George's Church in Esher, Surrey, a small village a few miles southwest of London. While there he fell in love with Susannah Garbrand, the maid of his patron, Francis Drake. The marriage took place in 1621.

After about six years at Esher, Hooker accepted a call in 1626 to be lecturer at the Church of St. Mary in Chelmsford, Essex. Chelmsford was a busy and prosperous market town about thirty miles northeast of London. As a lecturer in an Anglican Church he was expected to preach on Sunday afternoons and market days.

From the start Hooker's powerful preaching drew large congregations, including some persons of lofty social rank. Cotton Mather recounts how an irreligious man and his friends plotted to attend Hooker's lecture in order to cause a serious disturbance. The troublemaker had not been there long "before the *quick and powerful word* of God, in the mouth of his faithful *Hooker,* pierced the soul of him; he came out with an awakened and a distressed soul, and by the further blessing of God upon Mr. *Hooker's* ministry, he arrived unto a true *conversion.*" The man later followed Hooker to America.

Hooker did not lack courage in his preaching. On a national day of fasting when speaking to a crowded congregation at Chelmsford he beseeched God to enlighten the King and place him on a pious course. Remarkably enough, this criticism of Charles I did not precipitate governmental persecution of him.

Serious trouble, however, soon befell him. William Laud, Bishop of London since 1628, decided to wage an all-out campaign against Puritans in his bishopric. His agents soon began a close surveillance of Puritan clergy. Among those watched was Hooker whose reputation as an influential Puritan preacher already had spread far. In May 1629 the vicar of nearby Braintree wrote to Laud about Hooker's enormous and pernicious influence and urged Laud to remove him from his position. Soon afterwards he was ordered to appear before Laud. He was warned to cease his Puritan practices and especially his preaching on topics forbidden by the Church.

Hooker, however, was so deeply committed to Puritanism that he could not alter his practices. It became obvious to him that arrest and possible imprisonment lay ahead if he continued as lecturer at St. Mary's. So, probably late in 1629, he slipped away to the nearby village of Little Baddow where he taught school in a house called "Cuckoos Farm." Serving as his assistant was young John

Eliot, later to become noted as a missionary to New England Indians.

Hooker Flees to Holland and then to New England

Apparently Hooker could not resist occasional opportunities to preach because Laud's agents soon renewed their persecution. To escape a trial in the dreaded Court of High Commission Hooker quickly fled to Holland. Here in turn he served fellow Puritans in Amsterdam, Delft and finally in Rotterdam. There he became a colleague of William Ames and Hugh Peter. He admired Ames greatly, and the feeling was reciprocated. Ames even called Hooker the finest preacher and disputant of all the scholars whom he had ever known.

As time passed Hooker's thoughts turned increasingly to the possibility of migration to America. Men of his principles had no foreseeable future in the Church of England. Even in tolerant Holland he saw little chance to exert constructive leadership since he and his followers constituted only a handful of English in a great sea of Dutchmen! From Massachusetts Bay Colony in New England came pleas from some of Hooker's old friends in the Chelmsford area to serve them in the New World.

In 1633 Hooker made the crucial decision to start life anew in New England. He quietly re-entered England to arrange some personal affairs. Mather quaintly describes what happened:

Returning into *England* in order to a further voyage, he [Mr. Hooker] was quickly scented by the pursevants [officers]; who at length got so far up with him, as to knock at the door of that very chamber, where he was now discoursing with Mr. *Stone;* who was now become his designed companion and assistent for the *New-English* enterprize. Mr. *Stone* was at that instant smoking of *tobacco;* for which Mr. *Hooker* had been reproving him, as being then used by few persons of sobriety; being also of a sudden and pleasant wit, he stept unto the door, with his pipe in his mouth, and such an air of speech and look, as gave him some credit with the officer. The officer demanded, *Whether Mr.* Hooker *were not there?* Mr. *Stone* replied with a braving sort of confidence, *What* Hooker? *Do you mean* Hooker *that lived once at* Chelmsford! The officer answered, *Yes, he!* Mr. *Stone* immediately, with a diversion like that which once helped *Athanasius,* made this true answer, *If it be he you look for, I saw him about an hour ago, at such an house in the town; you had*

10

best hasten thither after him. The officer took this for a sufficient account, and went his way; but Mr. *Hooker*, upon this intimation, concealed himself more carefully and securely, till he went on board, at the *Downs*, in the year 1633, the ship which brought him, and Mr. *Cotton*, and Mr. *Stone* to *New-England*: where none but Mr. *Stone* was owned for a preacher, at their first coming aboard; the other two delaying to take their turns in the publick worship of the ship, till they were got so far into the main ocean, that they might with safety, discover who they were.

The presence of three leading Puritan ministers—John Cotton, Thomas Hooker and Thomas Stone—on one ship resulted in a veritable feast of preaching for the passengers! Each day during the eight weeks' crossing the 200 appreciative passengers enjoyed a sermon from one of the trio. Among the listeners was John Haynes, later to be a governor of Connecticut.

Soon after his arrival in Boston, September 4, 1633, Hooker with his assistant Stone journeyed to nearby Newtown (Cambridge) where a ready-made congregation eagerly awaited him. Soon afterwards they assumed the positions of pastor and teacher respectively. Newtown already was a substantial town with some inhabitants of affluence, and Hooker quickly won a position of leadership in the colony.

When Roger Williams came to trial in October 1635, Hooker was chosen to refute Williams' heretical stand on such issues as the charter, the freeman's oath, the free church and separatism. Each man argued most persuasively, but neither convinced the other. Public opinion, in general, supported Hooker so Williams was soon banished.

The Irresistible Lure of the Connecticut Valley

Hooker's Newtown contingent soon began to agitate for more land or emigration. In September 1634 they submitted a petition to the Massachusetts General Court. In it they cited three reasons for acquiring more land or leaving:(1) inadequate land for cattle, maintenance of ministers and new settlers; (2) abundant fertile land in Connecticut and Dutch designs on it; (3) "the strong bent of their spirits to remove thither." A hot debate developed before the Newtown group finally won the promise of additional land.

What really caused the Newtown group's desire to leave Mas-

11

sachusetts? There must have been more than meets the eye in the petition. The early historian, William Hubbard, may have gone to the heart of the problem when he wrote: "Two such eminent stars, such as were Mr. Cotton and Mr. Hooker, both of the first magnitude, though of differing influence, could not well continue in one and the same orb." Some policy differences had arisen between the two men, and Hooker may have felt that he never could be entirely his own man in Massachusetts where Cotton had preempted the role of chief clergyman.

For the great majority of would-be migrants to the Connecticut Valley the chief motivation clearly was economic not religious. They held essentially the same beliefs and worshipped in the same manner as most other residents of Massachusetts. The real attraction of Connecticut lay in the reports of abundant fertile land.

In 1635 the General Court reluctantly approved a renewed petition to depart for the Connecticut Valley provided the emigrants remained under Massachusetts rule. The lure of the valley thus proved irresistible to a substantial number of Massachusetts Bay people and likewise to other Englishmen in Plymouth and to some Dutchmen as well.

References Consulted*

Charles M. Andrews, *The Colonial Period of American History*, I, II (New Haven, 1934, 1936)

Maurice P. Ashley, *England in the Seventeenth Century* (London, 1952)

John Bruce, ed., *Calendar of State Papers, Domestic Series . . . 1628-29* (London, 1859)

Helen Cam, *England before Elizabeth* (London, 1950)

Marshall M. Knappen, *Tudor Puritanism* (Chicago, 1939)

Cotton Mather, *Magnalia Christi Americana . . .* I (Hartford, 1820)

John E. Neale, *Queen Elizabeth* (London, 1934)

Wallace Notestein, *The English People on the Eve of Colonization, 1603-1630* (New York, 1954)

Conyers Read, *The Tudors* (New York, 1936)

Alan Simpson, *Puritanism in Old and New England* (Chicago, 1955)

George L. Walker, *Thomas Hooker: Preacher, Founder, Democrat* (New York, 1891)

James K. Hosmer, ed., *Winthrop's Journal . . .* I (New York, 1908)

*Each chapter list includes works selected from the more important ones employed in preparation of the chapter.

II The Land and Its Original Inhabitants

Water—the Key to Success

When the first Dutch and English explorers viewed the lower Connecticut River Valley, they were elated with what they saw. The broad Connecticut River, except for a few sand bars, offered easy access to the interior. Above the Narrows at Middletown the valley broadened out and the soil appeared to be fertile. Six miles above Hartford were rapids at the future Enfield, but above the rapids were more miles of navigable stream. The Connecticut River, indeed, provided the key to the River Colony's rapid expansion. It offered easy ingress and egress, a highway for the new settlers and for the export of their surplus products. Without the great river it is difficult to imagine the rapid growth which actually occurred.

Water largely explains the early history of both the River Colony and the New Haven Colony. Connecticut had a drowned irregular coastline with many sheltered harbors, of which New London was the finest. In July 1680 the colony's leaders, answering an English query about harbors, declared that in New London "Ships of great burthen may com up to the town and lye secure in any winds." Later they wrote of "New London or Pequot River, wher a ship of 500 tunn may go up to the Towne, and com so near the shore that they may toss a biskit ashoare: and vessells of about 30 tunn may pass up about 12 miles above N. London, to or neer a town called Norwich."

Ships of up to 300 tons used New Haven and Fairfield harbors while small craft of thirty or forty tons put in at Guilford, Milford, Stratford, Norwalk and Stamford. The many harbors encouraged fishing, shipbuilding and trading.

Connecticut's Topography

Topographically Connecticut contained many hills, deep forests, ravines, rocks, rivers and over 1,000 lakes. If one excludes the later western land claims, Connecticut consisted of about 5,000 square miles—not a large area even in the seventeenth century. When the disputed boundaries finally were adjudicated, the eastern

13

line, with Rhode Island, totaled about 50 miles; that on Long Island Sound, nearly 100; the western, with New York, about 75; and the northern, with Massachusetts, 87. The early settlers had to look hard to find much flat terrain. On the coast was a narrow coastal plain. Along some rivers, especially the Connecticut above Middletown, were narrow plains with fertile soils. The spring floods, especially on the Connecticut, deposited some fertile silt on the adjacent bottom lands. The relatively deep rich alluvial soil of the central valley has made over 300 years of successful farming possible. Even the central valley is not large—only ten to twenty miles wide—and is punctuated here and there by small traprock peaks such as the Hanging Hills of Meriden, Mount Higby and Beseck Mountain.

To round out the topographic features of Connecticut, the early settlers found to the east and west of the great valley long low ranges of hills known later as the Eastern and Western Highlands. As one moves northward the altitude gradually increases to about 1,300 feet in northeastern Connecticut and to 2,380 feet on Mount Frissell in the northwestern corner. The highest area, including Mount Frissell and Bear Mountain, belongs to the Taconic range of mountains. While the highlands provide scenery attractive to modern dwellers and visitors, they chiefly afforded the early farmers back-breaking toil on thin rocky soils which tended to erode badly and wear out rapidly.

Throughout Connecticut the land was mostly covered with magnificent virgin forests broken here and there by Indian clearings. Large stands of such coniferous (soft wood) trees as balsam, cedar, hemlock and pine dotted the land. Among the deciduous (hard wood) trees were ash, basswood, beech, birch, buttonwood, chestnut, elm, hickory, maple, oak, pepperidge, poplar, sassafras, sycamore, walnut, whitewood and wild cherry. The pioneers especially prized the oak, pine and whitewood. Out of whitewood, for instance, they made superior boards and clapboards for their houses. The forests tended to have far less underbrush than today because Indians often burned it off to trap deer and other game.

The hunter of today must envy the early colonial hunters who could shoot wild turkey, heron, partridge, quail and pigeons. Bear, deer, fox, mink, otter, wild cat and wolf were abundant. So feared

14

was the wolf that as early as May 1647 a bounty of ten shillings was offered for killing one—an incentive repeated in the Code of 1650.

Both Indians and whites reveled in the abundance of water-fowl and fish. Most of the rivers teemed with fish. In the Connecticut River salmon and shad were special delights. Along the shores settlers easily obtained clams, lobsters, oysters and shellfish. Ducks, broadbills, teal, sheldrake, wigeons and wild geese flourished in the lakes, rivers and coastal bays.

Every river and brook in Connecticut had its fall line within the colony so abundant waterpower was available. In most new towns one of the first rights granted was that for a gristmill.

Profound Geologic Changes

Connecticut's irregular terrain results from complex geologic changes occurring over hundreds of millions of years. In the beginning the land was covered by seas. Near the end of the Archeozoic age, perhaps more than a billion years ago, marine deposits were folded to create high mountains. By the mid-Paleozoic era, perhaps 400,000,000 years ago, the land rose and huge earthquakes ravaged the New England area. Most Connecticut rocks date from this era though the superficial surface characteristics reflect changes of later Mesozoic and Cenozoic periods. The lofty mountains of the late Paleozoic times towered over the country and disgorged avalanches from their snowy and icy sides. Upon arrival of the Mesozoic era, approximately 200,000,000 years ago, the slow erosion of mountains began. By the end of this era the large mountains had disappeared and the surface constituted a rolling peneplain with sluggish streams. The large central lowland of Triassic sandstone was mostly created during the mid-Mesozoic era.

When the Cenozoic period began, about 60,000,000 years ago, Connecticut experienced the Tertiary uplift. The land surface became elevated in a fairly even incline with the highest part in the northwestern corner. This action stimulated the rivers to a new cycle of erosion as they cut into hard crystalline rocks. The softer sandstones of the central valley yielded more rapidly and river terraces were formed. Modern Hartford rests on one of these terraces.

The final great geologic force which completed the task of

15

shaping Connecticut's topography was glaciation. The climate became extremely cold as huge sheets of ice—hundreds of feet thick—moved inexorably southward over Connecticut. The great weight of the ice carried enormous quantities of soil, stones and even bedrock. Much of our soil ended in Long Island Sound, but in turn, soil and boulders from northern New England were deposited here. Over thousands of years the climate gradually warmed up and the ice slowly melted. The earlier valleys and highlands were little affected by the glaciers, although they moved soil around, rounded the tops of hills and scratched, gouged and polished rocks forming striae. As the glaciers melted, loose material accumulated in small hills or drumlins—especially in the northeast. In addition, the melting glaciers formed sand plains, clay beds and serpentine ridges. In several cases the glacial debris radically altered a river's course. The Farmington River, which once flowed southward into the Sound at New Haven, was diverted northward through an ancient gap at Tariffville and then easterly to the Connecticut River at Windsor. The glacier scoured out a rock hole 108 feet deep—whose bottom is 82 feet below sea level—now known as Lake Saltonstall. By destroying drainage patterns the glacier formed most of the more than 1,000 lakes and 400 swamps in Connecticut. While glaciers carried off much topsoil, they vastly enriched the land with hundreds of beautiful lakes and ponds, lovely waterfalls, picturesque drumlins, ridges and boulders as well as fine harbors. There can be no doubt that they added greatly to the charm of Connecticut's landscape.

The early settlers enjoyed one great asset envied by modern man—sparkling clean air and water. Without the pollutants of industrialized society Indians and whites breathed pure air, drank clean water and had no reason to worry about the ecology of their country.

Connecticut's Indians

When Thomas Hooker reached Hartford in 1636, there were perhaps 6,000 or 7,000 Indians in Connecticut. The population probably was much larger earlier, but a deadly plague in 1616-17 killed thousands of New England Indians. They were thickest along the coast, perhaps because fishing offered an easier and more

16

reliable subsistence than hunting. Even along the coast, however, their population was relatively low. In 1638 the Quinnipiacs, residents of the attractive area from Milford to Madison, told John Davenport that they had only forty-seven men—which translated into about 250 persons for the tribe. Even the Pequots, most dreaded of all local Indians, could marshal only 500 to 600 warriors. Yet the Indians greatly outnumbered the Puritans for a number of years, and had the potential power to annihilate them.

All of the tribes belonged to the loose Algonkin confederation, but they constantly quarreled with each other, allowing the whites to play one tribe against another. While each tribe apparently spoke a different tongue, there were enough similarities that members of different Connecticut tribes could understand each other. J. Hammond Trumbull in his famous study of Indian languages described four distinct Algonkin dialects in Connecticut and nearby areas: (1) Pequot-Mohegan; (2) Niantic and Narraganset (into Rhode Island, also); (3) Nipmuck (into Massachusetts); and (4) Quinipi (Quinnipiac).

Precise well-documented information about Connecticut Indians and their civilization is tantalizingly fragmentary. They left no written records so we are dependent for information on archaeological evidence and writings of contemporary whites who observed their customs and culture. While there is little documented evidence about the origins of North American Indians, most scholars agree that they crossed the Bering Straits from Asia about 10,000 or 11,000 years ago. In Connecticut investigations have been made in at least eighty archaeological sites, but the picture obtained of Indian culture has been frustratingly incomplete.

Despite this, certain generalizations seem valid. Both archaeological and contemporary historical accounts indicate that the local Indians practiced far more than a hunting-fishing economy. Vegetable products seem to have ranked first among foods, with fish and shellfish second, and mammals and birds, third. This shift from "hunter-gatherer" to horticulturist occurred in Connecticut about 1,000 A.D. if the local situation paralleled that in New York —which probably was the case.

Maize (Indian corn) appears to have comprised the mainstay of Indian diet, and was eaten in porridge and unleavened cakes.

17

They also enjoyed maize boiled on the ear, roasted and even popped. They relished succotash—a mixture of maize and beans boiled together in an earthen pot. Sometimes the mixture was seasoned with fish, or with ground nuts and artichokes, thickened with a flour formed from powdered nuts. Much maize was turned into cornmeal and hominy. For winter's use they stored dried maize and fish in large pits. Women seem to have performed most of the labor in planting, cultivating and harvesting the crops. Indians capitalized on various noncultivated foods such as acorns, chestnuts, walnuts, currants, huckleberries, plums and strawberries.

Many kinds of fish and shellfish were caught by Connecticut's Indians. While the archaeological and ethnographic reports particularly stress sturgeon, many other varieties are mentioned including bass, bluefish, bream, carp, catfish, cod, haddock, hake, halibut, herring, mackerel, pickerel, pike, salmon, shad, smelt and swordfish. They employed several methods of fishing including lines to harpoon them by means of a sharp jagged bone. Also, they used weirs. Women and children searched the coasts for lobsters, clams and other shellfish. Archaeological sites consistently reveal shellfish remains.

The hunting prowess of the Indian is legendary. Archaeological sites indicate that the white-tailed deer probably contributed the most meat to the Indian diet. Connecticut Indians hunted deer with bow and arrow, as well as traps. Deerhunting season seems to have been in fall and winter. Like modern deerhunters they preferred ample snow cover for tracking and slowing them down. Early writers on Indians agree that the next most frequently hunted animal was the bear. Indians succeeded by various methods—bow and arrow, traps and surrounding the lair and hatcheting the hibernating animal. They also hunted the beaver and otter for their warm skins, and the wolf because they considered it a dangerous pest.

Connecticut Indians like all those in New England were basically stationary in that each tribe remained within recognized tribal lands. Within this fixed area they moved about according to weather and food sources. Because of their desire to move fairly frequently their homes were of light construction and easily built and dismantled. At times they would move to the coast and enjoy fishing. As bitter weather approached they might withdraw into a

18

sheltered valley amply supplied with firewood. Some tribes had fortified villages. The houses were usually located very close to each other, but a space was reserved in the center for ceremonies and public business. To build a house poles were set in the ground, bent together and fastened at the top. Daniel Gookin, writing in 1674, described their houses as usually twenty to forty feet long, but occasionally as much as one hundred feet long and thirty feet wide. The better houses were carefully covered with bark and stayed very warm. Reeds and rushes often were used to thatch the roof. Around the fortified village was a solid barrier of young trees firmly entrenched in the earth and forming a palisade ten to twelve feet high. At the ends the fence overlapped to form a narrow passage which was blocked at night by piles of brushwood.

The furnishings of the typical house were extremely simple. John DeForest claims that Indians had advanced enough to have bedsteads constructed of light framework and covered with skins. Crude wooden bowls made from hard woods, baskets often tastefully decorated, pails, pots and bowls of baked earth often with pointed bottoms and large wooden spoons constituted the majority of the implements in daily use.

In New England tribes the medicine man or powwow played an influential role. He was thought to possess supernatural powers. Since Indians had little medicine as such they relied heavily on the medicine man to rout evil spirits from the body.

Algonkin religions varied among tribes but shared a lack of systematic dogma or scriptures. Roger Williams and John Eliot who came to know the Indians intimately asserted they believed the soul immortal though they could not grasp resurrection in the Christian meaning.

Among the important Indian contributions to Connecticut was the name "Connecticut" itself. In the Algonkin language *Quinnetukut* and variants such as *Quenticutt, Quinetucquet* and *Quanehta-cut* all meant "on the long tidal river," an appropriate name for the area. "Connecticut" simply represented in writing what the early colonists thought they heard the Indians saying.

Location of the Various Tribes

When the whites arrived in Connecticut, there were about

Map of Indian trails, tribes and villages.

Courtesy of Connecticut State Library. Photo by Clarence Casabella

20

sixteen separate Indian tribes. In central Connecticut lived the Podunks whose village Adriaen Block visited in 1614. In 1631 Wahginnacut, a Podunk chief, visited Plymouth and Boston describing the beauty and trading potential of the Connecticut Valley. They strongly desired English settlers as protection against the Pequots. The Podunks dwelled along the Connecticut River from modern Warehouse Point to Manchester and Glastonbury and inland to Bolton and Vernon.

In Hartford Hooker's company encountered the Saukiogs, ruled by Sequassen. In 1636 he sold all of the future Hartford and West Hartford to the English. Because of recent defeats by the Pequots and Mohegans the Saukiogs cultivated the friendship of the colonists. Sequassen himself later became angered by the English alliance with Uncas and supposedly hired an assassin to kill Governor John Haynes, Governor Edward Hopkins and William Whiting. Apparently he intended to blame Uncas and the Mohegans for the murder. The plot miscarried, Sequassen fled, and the Mohegans carried him to Hartford for trial. Since the plot could not be proved, however, Sequassen was freed. There is a possibility that Uncas himself may have engineered the entire plot.

Farther south at Pyquag (Wethersfield) lived the Wangunks with their sachem Sequin, father of Sequassen. The tribe controlled an area from Wethersfield and Middletown east to East Hampton, south to Haddam and west to Berlin and Meriden.

In the northeast, centered in Massachusetts, resided the Nipmucks. Many, however, lived in the future Somers, Stafford, Union, Woodstock, Thompson and Putnam. Quite peaceable by nature, they tended to be dominated by neighboring tribes. One of these just to their south was the Mohegans. They had recently split from the Pequots because Uncas, rejected as Pequot chieftain, led a walkout to the north. Uncas seems to have been a perpetual agitator and plotter who managed to keep Indians and whites constantly embroiled in dissensions. The Mohegans certainly ranked with the Pequots as one of the most powerful tribes in Connecticut.

The Pequots inhabited the southeast coastal corner of Connecticut with their strength concentrated in the Mystic River section. Recent migrants from the Hudson River region, they had moved southeasterly bisecting the Nehantics (Niantics). Because

21

of their highly aggressive and bellicose temperament they later challenged the white settlers.

Along the Sound west of the Pequots and Nehantics dwelt at least five small friendly tribes: (1) the Hammonassets in the Saybrook-Clinton area; (2) the Menunketucks in Guilford and Madison; (3) the Quinnipiacs around New Haven; (4) the Paugussetts located in Bridgeport, Stratford and Waterbury; and (5) the Siwanogs extending from Stamford to Greenwich and inland to Ridgefield, Wilton and New Canaan.

Near the Saukiogs in northern Connecticut lived the Poquonocks around Windsor, Bloomfield and East Granby and the Tunxis in Farmington, New Britain and Berlin. Along the river and westward, a spillover from Massachusetts to Enfield, Suffield, Hartland and Granby, were the Agawams. Their neighbors to the southwest were the Massacoes in Weatogue, Canton, Simsbury and parts of Granby, East Granby and Barkhamsted.

Most of western and northwestern Connecticut was uninhabited except for occasional fierce Mohawk hunters from New York. Later as the Mohawks developed a genuine respect for the strength of the whites they gradually ceased their aggressive incursions into Connecticut. Remnants of several Connecticut tribes eventually moved into the New Milford-Kent area and organized as a new tribe—the Scatacooks.

Anthropological research has revealed that the Connecticut Indians were influenced culturally by their powerful western neighbors, the Mohawks, and the Iroquois confederacy in general. Their architecture, basketry, ceramics, costumes, decorative designs, embroidery and implements all reflect the great influence of the Iroquois. Although Connecticut Indians greatly feared the Mohawks, they carefully imitated their culture.

References Consulted

Thomas A. Cook, *Geology of Connecticut* (Hartford, 1933)

William S. Dakin, *Geography of Connecticut* (Boston, 1926)

John W. DeForest, *History of the Indians of Connecticut* (Hartford, 1853)

Richard F. Flint, *The Glacial Geology of Connecticut* (Hartford, 1930)

Charles J. Hoadly, ed., *The Public Records of the Colony of Connecticut* . . . IV (Hartford, 1868)

Albert L. Olson, *Agricultural Economy and the Population in Eighteenth-Century Connecticut*, Connecticut Tercentenary Commission Publications, No. 40 (New Haven, 1935)

William N. Rice, *The Physical Geography and Geology of Connecticut* (Hartford, 1904)

Benjamin Trumbull, *A Complete History of Connecticut* . . . (New London, 1898)

James Hammond Trumbull, "The Composition of Indian Geographical Names, Illustrated from the Algonkin Languages," Connecticut Historical Society *Collections*, II (Hartford, 1870)

Frederick W. Warner, "Some Aspects of Connecticut Indian Culture History" (Unpublished Ph.D. dissertation, Hartford Seminary Foundation, 1970)

III The Pioneer White Settlers of Connecticut

The Dutch Vie with the English

In 1614 a Dutchman, Adriaen Block, and a few companions sailed up the unexplored Connecticut River in a small boat just forty-four and one-half feet long. They reached the site of the future Hartford and may have gone as far north as the falls at Enfield. The first whites known to have explored the river, they named it the Fresh River or Fresh Water.

For a number of years the Dutch were content to carry on a trade in beaver skins with Indians along the river. In the 1620's plans were drawn up for fortified posts, and the first site acquired at the mouth of the river was named Kievit's Hoeck. A few years later on June 8, 1633, Jacob Van Curler bought from the Pequots, owners by conquest, a small piece of land where the city of Hartford is now located. The Dutch moved rapidly to build a small fort, named it the House of Good Hope and invited Indian trade.

The Dutch narrowly won the race for first white settlement in the Hartford area. Highly encouraging reports on the fertility of the Connecticut River Valley had reached both the Plymouth and Boston areas in 1631 from visiting Indians who feared the Pequot tribe. Intrigued by these glowing reports, in 1632 Edward Winslow of Plymouth explored the Connecticut River to ascertain the possibilities for fur trade and actual colonization.

Encouraged by Winslow's optimistic description of the area, the Plymouth Colony sent a small expedition under William Holmes to do some trading. When he reached a point opposite the Dutch fort, they brusquely ordered him to stop while they investigated his intentions. Unruffled, he announced that he had a Plymouth commission authorizing him to proceed upstream to trade. Despite Dutch threats to blow them up, Holmes and his men moved forward unharmed. On September 26, 1633, the Holmes company reached a location, purchased earlier from Indians, where they set up a house frame carried from Plymouth. Around it they erected a stockade to ward off possible Indian or Dutch encroachment. Thus Windsor was founded.

24

The Dutch did not allow this direct challenge to go unanswered. They sent seventy men against the little settlement, but encountered such a resolute defense that they withdrew without firing a shot. Later the Dutch tried to locate a settlement upstream from Windsor, but a smallpox epidemic among the Indians foiled the plan.

Neither the Dutch nor the Plymouth group remained in control of the area for long as many new settlers arrived the next few years. One of these groups came from Dorchester, Massachusetts. This band of people originally sailed from Plymouth, England, in 1630 under two ministers—John Maverick and John Warham. Among their lay leaders were Edward Rossiter, Roger Ludlow and John Mason. This select company, numbering 140 in all, arrived at Nantasket on May 30, 1630. Soon afterwards they settled at nearby Dorchester.

In the summer of 1635 a vanguard of this group settled at Windsor near the Plymouth group. In November an additional sixty men, women and children, plus livestock, reached Windsor. The fates were most unkind and winter arrived unbelievably early. By mid-November the river had frozen over and expected provisions could not get through. Fearing starvation a few fled by land back to Massachusetts. Actually facing starvation, many of the others went to the river's mouth looking for their provisions ship. Not finding it, they went aboard the *Rebecca*, a vessel temporarily frozen in the ice. A providential rain fell, freeing them, and the half-starved, demoralized pioneers sailed to Boston. The few brave souls who dared to remain in Windsor suffered appallingly. Somehow by hunting and begging aid from friendly Indians they survived the winter though many of their cattle died.

The next spring Warham and others arrived and swelled the total to more than one-half the original population of Dorchester. Ignoring the Plymouth title to Windsor, they proceeded to erect houses on high ground above the river. Their action in occupying part of the land Plymouth purchased from the Indians created much bitterness. The Plymouth settlers complained with much justification that they had gone to great trouble and expense in establishing the Windsor settlement. Yet nothing could be done about the interlopers. Massachusetts Bay Colony's resources greatly exceeded those of Plymouth. Eventually, after an acrimonious dispute, the matter was settled in 1637 by Plymouth selling most of its Connecticut land to the Dorchester group. A residue of ill will continued for many years.

Founding of Wethersfield and Hartford

Meanwhile Wethersfield, the second of the English river towns, had been started, though there is uncertainty about the exact date of its founding. In 1633 John Oldham, the restless adventurer of Dorchester, visited the Connecticut River and traded with the Indians. He may have visited the future site of Wethersfield. In the fall of 1634 he and eight or nine companions came to Pyquag (Indian name for Wethersfield) where they built temporary houses for the winter. Oldham himself, always on the move, probably soon left. The next spring brought settlers from Watertown, Massachusetts. In 1635 and 1636 about thirty Watertown families arrived and were augmented by others, including a few directly from England. Unlike Windsor and Hartford which were settled by large church groups as *units*, Wethersfield was established much more by *individuals* with no official connections to Massachusetts.

The most renowned of the three original river settlements—Hartford—was founded last. In June 1636 Hooker's company left Newtown and spent about two weeks migrating to Hartford. About 100 people and 160 head of cattle plus goats and pigs comprised the company.

This group came last because they were the most careful in obtaining legal clearance from the Massachusetts Bay government. From a strict legal viewpoint all of the 1633-35 settlers were simply squatters. The best title to Connecticut land at that time was the Warwick Patent. In 1632 Robert, Earl of Warwick, conveyed to certain men a large amount of land in New England including Connecticut. The patent merely bestowed land and did not grant governmental powers or create a corporation.

In 1635 six of the grantees persuaded John Winthrop, Jr., to establish a colony in Connecticut with him as governor. In November he sent about twenty men to make a settlement at Saybrook, though he did not come until April 1636. The following March a fort was erected by Lion Gardiner, a skilled engineer. He had come to Saybrook with a commission from the Fenwick group to direct the defense of the mouth of the river.

Saybrook's establishment posed a challenge to the Hooker company. Eventually a clever compromise was achieved whereby Hooker and associates recognized the Warwick claims as legal and acknowledged Winthrop as governor. In return, Winthrop and associates approved the proposed Hooker settlement. Both groups then approached the Massachusetts General Court for a specific enactment. On March 3, 1635/36, the Court issued a commission authorizing eight men, who were in Connecticut or about to go, to govern, establish courts and even wage war. They were empowered to convene inhabitants of the towns to act as a general court. So at last Connecticut's river settlements seemed to have a legal basis!

The Pequots Threaten the Infant Colony

The single exception to the rule of Indian-white friendship was the Pequots. The trouble began between the Pequots and the Dutch. Some Indians trading with the Dutch were killed by Pequots. The Dutch, seeking revenge, accidentally killed Wopigwooit, a Pequot chieftain. The Pequots, in turn, sought revenge on the first whites to present themselves and wiped out a small group of traders under Captain John Stone of Virginia.

After this the Pequots became concerned about their reputation. They wanted trade with the colonists so they sent two sets of emissaries to Boston with presents and pledges of good behavior. Eventually an agreement was concluded by which the Pequots promised to turn over the slayers of Stone's party and allow the English to have freedom of settlement in Connecticut. For their part the English agreed to a friendly trade with the Pequots.

Peace was short-lived. In 1636 John Oldham set out on a trading expedition to Long Island Sound. Near Block Island Indians suddenly attacked and brutally killed him. The murder produced horror in Boston where demands for quick revenge sounded. A careful investigation revealed that Block Island Indians were guilty, but the Pequots had provided them refuge. Therefore an expedition of ninety men under Captain John Endecott set out for Block Island. The Indians escaped but much property was destroyed.

Then Endecott's forces went to Saybrook. Lion Gardiner pleaded with them not to attack the Pequots because, as he worded it, "you come hith[e]r to raise thes wasps about my eares, and then you will take wing and flee away." Gardiner was only too correct in his prediction. The expedition failed to force a battle and settled for large-scale ravaging of crops, canoes and wigwams. The infuriated Pequots hardly could wait to wreak vengeance.

As the first step in a design to eliminate all English settlements in Connecticut, the Pequots began a nearly continuous siege of the Saybrook fort. To intimidate the whites, the Indians, keeping themselves just out of range, "would imitate the dying Groans and Invocations of the poor Captive English." During the siege Lion Gardiner's son, David, was born on April 29, 1636—the first recorded white birth in Connecticut.

The Pequot danger increased greatly through their plans for a close alliance with the Narragansets. This so alarmed the Boston authorities that they asked Roger Williams for aid in preventing it. Although Williams had suffered banishment at the hands of Massachusetts, he immediately set out by canoe through stormy seas to visit the Narragansets. While the extent of his influence is uncertain, it is entirely possible that his intervention was crucial in their decision not to ally with the Pequots.

As if the siege of Saybrook, the murder of Oldham and the wooing of the Narragansets were not enough evidence of the Pequots' hostility, they soon provided more. In April 1637 a band of Pequots surprised a group of whites working in a meadow along the river at Wethersfield. In a brief but sanguinary engagement at least six men and three women were killed and two young women seized. Making their escape downstream the Pequots celebrated the event as they passed Saybrook fort by waving some of their victims' clothes on poles!

Outbreak of War Against the Pequots

In the river towns many felt they no longer could tolerate the Pequot menace. On May 1, 1637, the General Court at Hartford voted to wage an offensive war and summoned ninety men—forty-two from Hartford, thirty from Windsor and eighteen from Wethersfield. They selected John Mason as commander and voted one hogshead of beer for the men. They assigned each town a quota of provisions.

While the expedition was being organized an unwelcome and embarrassing offer of assistance came from Uncas. After his separation from the Pequots he had been seeking a chance to overthrow Sassacus, the Pequot chieftain. Uncas nurtured great ambitions to regain control of the Pequots and even oust Miantonomo, the chief of the Narragansets. Through an alliance with the English he saw the opportunity to reach his goals. His offer of the services of himself and eighty warriors caused very mixed reactions. Despite strong objections, Mason insisted on acceptance.

In mid-May the joint expedition left Hartford. Uncas and his Mohegans got permission to go on ahead to Saybrook where Gardiner received them with considerable suspicion. Determined to test their loyalty, he asked them to send twenty warriors after six Pequots who had passed the previous night. The Pequots must be brought back dead or alive, or he would dissolve the alliance. When they killed four Pequots and took one prisoner, Gardiner was convinced.

Upon Mason's arrival at Saybrook a serious discussion on future strategy took place. Most of the men wanted to attack the Pequots directly. Captain Mason, impressed by the great dangers involved in a direct assault against superior numbers of Pequots at the Mystic River, proposed an attack from the rear via Narragansett Bay. Because of much intense opposition to the plan the group asked the chaplain, the Reverend Thomas Stone, to seek divine guidance. After spending the night in prayer, he told the men the next morning that he felt divine approval had been indicated. So the Narragansett Bay plan was adopted and nineteen Massachusetts men under Captain Underhill joined forces.

The small fleet then sailed past the Pequot harbor where the jeering Pequots assumed that the palefaces lacked courage to attack them. In an exultant mood the Pequots made plans for further attacks against the river towns.

When Mason's expedition arrived in Narraganset territory, they received a cordial welcome. Miantonomo, however, warned them of the Pequots' great prowess. To Mason's delight a band of Narragansets volunteered for service and joined in the march

29

westward. For some peculiar reason the nearer the little army came to the Pequots the lower the enthusiasm of the Narragansets for attack and the more they fell behind! When Mason learned that the Pequots held two forts, he determined to attack the nearer one. In the distance he and his men could hear the Pequots singing "until Midnight, with great Insulting and Rejoycing."

A Surprise for the Pequots

Later in the night the men marched close to the Pequot fort, which was surrounded by a wall of logs standing on end. Inside on each side of a middle lane stood many huts with roofs composed of straw mats. Mason and his men crept silently toward one gate while Underhill and his force approached the other. As Mason arrived within fifteen feet of an entrance a dog barked and an Indian cried *"Owanux,"* meaning *"Englishmen."* The force rushed the gate with Mason leading the way over a brush pile. Seeing no Indians inside Mason ran into a wigwam. Immediately Indians sprang up around him. At this moment, one of his soldiers entered the wigwam and created enough confusion so Mason escaped. Outside he reorganized his forces at each end of the fort. Although the Indians were dazed, they still much outnumbered the whites. Seizing a firebrand from a wigwam Mason threw it into the roof mat. It caught and a strong wind spread flames over the fort. Mason and his men escaped and tightened their ring around the fort. Most of the Pequots either died in the flames or were slain outside. In this surprisingly complete victory Mason saw the working of God's will. Most modern readers are more likely to react with feelings of great horror.

For the victorious Mason forces the moment actually was one of great danger. Sassacus and his warriors from the second fort had learned of the attack. The Narragansets had deserted, leaving the whites and Mohegans to face an infuriated foe. Moreover, twenty men were needed to carry a few badly wounded soldiers so only about forty whites remained. They hurried toward the shore uncertain when their boats would arrive. Suddenly in the distance they saw their vessels entering the harbor just as 300 Pequots approached. Mason audaciously attacked them with a small detachment. This temporarily checked the Pequots while Mason's force resumed its retreat to their boats. The Pequots then discovered that their fort was incinerated and shouting epithets they resumed the pursuit. Once again the rear guard fired and halted the onrush. Soon afterwards the Pequots abandoned the action. Mason's expedition had scored a complete triumph!

This catastrophic defeat produced an internal crisis within the Pequot tribe. Many members blamed Sassacus for the defeat and some even advocated killing him. In a tribal council three courses were debated: (1) a revenge attack against the English; (2) the same against the Narragansets; or (3) flight westward. Sassacus wished to fight, but those favoring flight won so the entire tribe retreated westward.

Meanwhile Mason's victorious army returned home to great acclamation. Two weeks later came news that Massachusetts' ships with 120 men under Captain Israel Stoughton had arrived to fight the Pequots. The General Court, meeting at Hartford on June 26, 1637, empowered John Haynes and Roger Ludlow to confer at Mystic Harbor with the Massachusetts spokesmen. In quick order this delegation agreed to pursue and attack the retreating Pequots.

Decimation of the Pequots

Meanwhile the terrified Pequots were moving very slowly because of the children and the need to secure food. As a result the white forces rapidly overtook them. Finally the pursuers sighted the Indians across a swamp in Fairfield. When the Pequots saw the enemy, they took refuge in the swamp.

The problem of how to destroy the Indian power necessitated a council of war. Some proposed surrounding the swamp before penetrating it. In all likelihood this would mean the death of many women and children. Thomas Stanton, competent in the Pequot language, offered to enter the swamp and negotiate with the Pequots. Many advised against such a hazardous venture, but Stanton insisted. Many expected to be killed. Hours later he walked out of the swamp followed by 200 women, children and old men.

That night Captains John Mason and Daniel Patrick (of Massachusetts) placed their forces to surround the swamp as completely as possible. Just before dawn the Pequots, shouting loudly, tried several times to break through the cordon before sixty or seventy finally knifed their way through. The remainder, except for a few slain, were captured—adding another 180 prisoners. The few who escaped suffered an even worse fate among Indians to the west. As a special mark of friendship the Mohawk Indians sent the head of Sassacus to Connecticut authorities.

The desperate Pequot survivors volunteered to become English subjects as the price for their lives. After a study of the situation the colonists divided the remnant among the Mohegans, Narragansets and Nehantics. The Pequots swore to renounce their name and their territory. The decimated remnant no longer existed as a real tribe and soon was only a vivid memory. If the Pequots had moved more swiftly and decisively against the colonists, it is entirely possible that they could have wiped out the River Colony. Instead, the settlers now had a military hero in John Mason and, more important, a feeling of security against Indian attack.

Springfield Lost but Other Towns Gained

In 1636 William Pynchon arrived with a few companions in two shallops at Springfield where they built a trading house, first on the west bank and later on the east. This settlement was thought by its founders to be a part of Connecticut. Located only twenty-four miles upstream from Hartford, Springfield logically should have remained in Connecticut.

Perhaps as a means of binding the Springfield settlement closer to the river towns the General Court voted Pynchon a monopoly of the Indian trade up the river in return for providing Indian corn. A month later the General Court, at a session attended by Pynchon, considered a complaint that he had not expanded the corn trade as much as expected and fined him forty bushels of corn. Never again did Pynchon attend the General Court.

Gradually the split between Pynchon and Connecticut deepened. Hooker strongly opposed Massachusetts' claim to Springfield and resented Pynchon's support for it. In economic matters the two areas varied sharply as Springfield emphasized fur trade; the lower towns, agriculture. In 1641 Massachusetts appointed Pynchon a magistrate and judge for Springfield. At the organization of the New England Confederation in 1643, Springfield joined as part of Massachusetts.

The Stanley-Whitman House (1660) in Farmington.

Connecticut found consolation for this loss in the addition of several new towns. On January 16, 1639/40, the General Court authorized six men to survey the Tunxis River area for possible settlement. A little later a small number of settlers journeyed ten miles over the hills west of Hartford to settle. In 1645 the River Colony officially renamed the Tunxis settlement Farmington.

Meanwhile another colony, Saybrook, was experiencing very difficult times. Appointed as governor was the highly talented John Winthrop, Jr. Unfortunately the restless Winthrop gave the infant colony little of his time or energies beyond procuring supplies. When the formidable Pequot threat became evident, Winthrop tried to negotiate with them but failed. At this critical juncture he suddenly abandoned the endangered colony and returned to Boston. Unquestionably this irresponsible desertion represented the nadir

33

of his eventful career for he had calculated the immediate prospects of Saybrook as minimal and cold-bloodedly decided to employ his skills in more promising fields.

Saybrook survived his defection, but for years made very slow progress as none of the Puritan "men of quality" who had planned to settle there came. In fact the colony remained merely a small trading fort. In 1639 George Fenwick, head of Saybrook Colony from 1639-44, received a distinguished delegation of River Colony leaders—Deputy Governor Roger Ludlow, Thomas Hooker and Thomas Wells—to discuss the proposed confederation with Massachusetts. In April 1644 Fenwick was elected a Connecticut magistrate. Late that year an agreement was consummated which for all practical purposes made Saybrook a part of the River Colony. Fenwick conveyed the fort and the land, but not the jurisdiction, to Connecticut's perpetual use. While it seems likely that the consent of all the other Saybrook grantees really was needed, it never was obtained. Fenwick returned permanently to England, held important posts under Cromwell and lost any serious interest in Saybrook. From December 1644 on, Saybrook operated as a town in the River Colony with full rights and responsibilities. The town's strategic location assured control of the lower Connecticut River.

Another very strategic location—the mouth of the Thames River—early attracted settlers. In 1642 the Court granted 500 acres to Captain Mason and 500 more to soldiers who had served under him in the Pequot War. In April 1642 the Court provided for a broader distribution of 10,000 acres, but the enterprising John Winthrop, Jr., managed to make the first white settlement there. In 1644 he obtained a Massachusetts grant "at or near Pequott." In 1645 he explored the ground around the mouth of the Thames and probably actually started a small settlement. Not until 1646, however, did most of the permanent settlers arrive. Winthrop remained cool and circumspect as he presided over a colony claimed by both Massachusetts and Connecticut. The New England Confederation considered the disputed jurisdiction and decided in favor of Connecticut. Winthrop received a warm welcome from the River Colony which in 1648 commissioned him a magistrate and in 1651 elected him an assistant in the small aristocratic upper house of the legislature. In 1658 the town's name officially changed from Pequot to New London. Aided by Connecticut's finest harbor and a growing agricultural hinterland, New London rapidly developed into an important seaport.

Evolving a Framework of Government

When the River Colony began, its government consisted of eight magistrates named by the Massachusetts General Court. Since the River Colony had no intention of remaining under Massachusetts' rule, this form of government constituted only a stopgap. Stimulated by the Pequot crisis, the three towns set up a General Court which held its first session on May 1, 1637. The membership of fifteen men consisted of nine elected from the three towns plus six magistrates chosen in turn by the nine.

Even this enlarged body provided only a legislature not an overall framework of government. Apparently the need for a genuine system of government greatly concerned Hooker, for he delivered an important sermon on May 31, 1638, in which he outlined certain basic principles:

I That the choice of public magistrates belongs unto the people, by God's own allowance.

II The privilege of election, which belongs to the people, therefore must not be exercised according to their humours, but according to the blessed will and law of God.

III They who have power to appoint officers and magistrates, it is in their power, also, to set the bounds and limitations of the power and place unto which they call them.

Hooker believed that successful government required "the free consent of the people."

It seems almost certain that Hooker's sermon deeply influenced those who later in 1638 devised the new governmental document. Unfortunately we lack information as to who worked on it and how it was adopted. The brevity and the logical organization of the final document suggest that an able lawyer authored it. At the time the only trained lawyer in the colony was Roger Ludlow of Windsor—educated at Balliol College, Oxford, and the Inner Temple, London. Probably the General Court approved the finished work.

The Fundamental Orders consisted of a preamble followed by eleven "orders." Hartford, Wethersfield and Windsor joined to-

35

gether to form "an Orderly and decent Gouerment established according to God to Order and dispose of the affayres of the people." This formed a *civil* covenant corresponding to the *religious* covenant adopted by each Congregational church.

The new frame of government provided for a General Court to convene each April and September. At the April session the qualified voters would elect a governor and at least six magistrates for a one-year term. No person could succeed himself as governor. This did not preclude choosing a popular person as governor alternate years, and John Haynes and Edward Hopkins alternated in the 1639-54 period, excepting one year. The governor had to belong to an approved congregation (no religious heretics or nonbelievers permitted!) and have experience as a magistrate.

Each of the three towns should elect four deputies and future towns would be entitled to whatever number the Court thought fit. No religious requirements for voting were established. While a deputy could speak freely for his town, the towns were required to obey all laws passed by the Court. Thus the supremacy of the General Court over the individual towns was clearly enunciated.

While the governor convened the Court, it could be dissolved only at its own behest. The magistrates with the governor composed a court to administer justice. Fear of overpowerful magistrates—stemming from the Massachusetts experience and Hooker's opposition—surfaced in several provisions. If the governor or a majority of the magistrates failed to convene the Court, the freemen could call a meeting on their own initiative.

The Fundamental Orders explained in some detail just how elections should be held and who could vote. For instance, only "admitted Inhabitants" could vote for the deputies from each town. At that time only adult males, who usually belonged to the local Puritan church, were "admitted." Certainly excluded from the franchise were all women, children, apprentices, indentured servants, Negroes and Indians. One definitely did *not* have to be a member of the Congregational Church to be "admitted," however. In case the General Court found the election in any town illegal it could order the holding of a new election.

The powers of the General Court were fairly broad: to make and repeal laws, levy taxes. admit freemen, grant undisposed lands to towns or persons, call into question any individual for misdemeanors and "deale in any other matter that concerns the good of this common welth exceptc clcction of Magestrats. . . ."

As a whole the Fundamental Orders constitute only a brief outline of government—much less detailed than New Haven's fundamentals of 1639 and 1643. No procedural rules were prescribed for the General Court, nor was there provision for a speaker. Moreover there was no division of executive, legislative, judicial and administrative authority.

The Fundamental Orders have been called such grandiose things as the world's first written constitution, and America's first democratic constitution. However, leading scholars have differed in their interpretation. Charles M. Andrews of Yale adopted a negative view on all such claims. He observed that the word "fundamental" was ordinarily used by New England Puritans to mean a general law. He believed that the authors of the Fundamental Orders did not conceive of them as an organic law. In fact they wcre considered fair game for frequent additions and alterations. In the opposite camp one finds such astute students of Connecticut history as George M. Dutcher of Wesleyan University and William M. Maltbie, Chief Justice of the Connecticut Supreme Court, 1930-50. Dutcher declared that the Fundamental Orders "with some amendment served the settlers as their constitution until they received the charter from Charles II in 1662." Judge Maltbie felt that Connecticut's leaders and people of the 1639-62 period considered them a constitution.

The latest study of the Fundamental Orders—Mary Jeanne Anderson Jones' *Congregational Commonwealth*—conceives the Orders "a formal written constitution." She sees them as realizing the Puritan ideal of making church and state "virtually synonymous." She makes no claims for them, however, as America's or the world's first written constitution. To this writer the Orders do not appear basic and organic enough to merit the title of "constitution" and "framework of government" seems more accurate.

Davenport and Eaton Plan a New Colony

A remarkably unified group of stanch Puritans founded New Haven in 1638. Their counterpart of Thomas Hooker was John

Davenport. As a young man he had received training at Oxford University and after a long interruption graduated. In time he took over the parish of St. Stephen's in the heart of London. As head of a parish of 1,400 communicants, he led an extremely active life. During the dangerous plague of 1625 he endeared himself to his parishioners by his visits to the afflicted.

With Laud's accession to the bishopric of London, Davenport's position became steadily more precarious. An unscrupulous assistant brought charges of disallowed Puritan practices against him. He managed to clear himself but certainly Laud's agents henceforth kept close surveillance over his activities. Various events in the 1628-33 period gradually undermined his hopes of reforming the Church of England. In 1633 both John Cotton and Hooker pressed him to join them in migration to America. Though moved by their entreaties, and now an ardent Puritan, he still refused.

The appointment of Laud as Archbishop of Canterbury in August 1633 crushed Davenport's final hopes. The next day he hurriedly left London and prepared for migration. About mid-November, disguised behind a large beard, wearing a gray suit and posing as a merchant, he crossed the Channel to Holland.

Like Hooker he found life in Holland uncongenial. After brief experiences in Amsterdam and Rotterdam he quietly returned to London. He found his former parish of St. Stephen's suffering and England badly rent by political and religious conflict. New England appeared to be the only solution to an intolerable situation.

At this moment his trusted friend, the merchant Theophilus Eaton, suddenly appeared. He had enjoyed a remarkably successful career in the Baltic trade but strong Puritan beliefs also pushed him toward America. With his wealth and business acumen he proved an ideal choice as the joint guiding force with Davenport in organizing a large group of colonists.

Working smoothly together Davenport and Eaton gathered their Puritan followers. The Eaton and Davenport families, some relatives, many St. Stephen's parishioners and about twenty families from the London neighborhood constituted the company. Puritans of the strictest type, many of them wealthy, the Davenport-Eaton group sought above all to found a true Bible State in New England.

The expedition sailed in May 1637. Apparently their safe arrival in Boston produced feelings of genuine joy as Governor Winthrop wrote in his *Journal* for June 26, 1637: "There arrived two ships from London, the *Hector* and the [blank]. In these came Mr. Davenport and another minister, and Mr. Eaton and Mr. Hopkins, two merchants of London, men of fair estate and of great esteem for religion, and wisdom in outward affairs."

The immediate concern of the new arrivals was to find a favorable site for permanent settlement. The Bay Colony offered various locations but none appealed to the group, dominated as it was by London merchants who wanted above all a good harbor.

Founding the Colony at New Haven

As a result of the Pequot War glowing reports came to Boston about Quinnipiac (New Haven) with its fertile land and fine harbor. Many thought it would be a great pity for so promising an area to fall into Dutch hands. Early in September Eaton and a few associates visited the Quinnipiac site which impressed them so highly that a few men apparently remained over the winter to hold their claim.

Eaton and his friends observed that they had found their Promised Land. Spurring them on further was the growing dissension within the Bay Colony, particularly Anne Hutchinson with her heretical ideas. This and other internal disaffection convinced the Davenport-Eaton company to create their own Bible State as rapidly as possible. Because of the smallness of the group they solicited volunteers. Among those accepting was the Reverend Peter Prudden, a graduate of Emmanuel College, Cambridge, and some Puritans from Hertfordshire.

On April 24, 1638, in the fresh beauty of early spring, the Puritan company landed on the shores of New Haven Bay. On the next day, a Sabbath, John Davenport convened his company under a huge oak tree where they heard him preach on an appropriate text from St. Matthew: "Then was Jesus led up of the spirit into the wilderness to be tempted of the devil." In the afternoon Mr. Prudden followed on the subject "The voice of one crying in the wilderness, Prepare ye the way of the Lord, make his paths straight."

The settlers found the nearby Indians friendly and by treaties signed in November and December 1638 and May 1645 were able to acquire large areas of land which covered coastal and inland areas, including the future Cheshire, Wallingford and parts of Orange, Bethany, Prospect, Woodbridge and Meriden. In the first treaty the Indians sold all their Quinnipiac lands, reserving hunting and fishing rights, for twelve coats of English cloth, twelve spoons, twelve hatchets, twelve hoes, two dozen knives, twelve porringers and four cases of French knives and scissors. The Indians were so impressed by Davenport's bookish habits that they called him *"So big study man."* White-Indian relations in this area were amicable— probably a direct outgrowth of a conscious attempt by the whites to deal fairly.

The center of New Haven took its distinctive form early when surveyor John Brockett divided the town plot into nine squares, with the center one reserved for a market place. It became the famous and still beautiful New Haven Green. The other eight squares soon proved inadequate in size and two "suburbs" were added.

Organizing a Strict Bible State

Not until 1639 did the New Haven Puritans formally move to organize their church. Citing the Scriptures as "a perfect rule" for men, they voted to select twelve men who in turn would choose seven as the founders of their permanent church and state. Named as the seven pillars were Davenport, Eaton, Jeremy Dixon, Thomas Fugill, Mathew Gilbert, Robert Newman and John Ponderson. The profession of faith of these seven indicated little doctrinal variance from the Church of England. The large differences were found in church government and form of service. The church covenant was completed in August 1639 and served as the model for later churches on the Sound.

The New Haven Colony differed sharply from the River Colony in that it required "that church members only shall be free burgesses, and thatt they onely shall chuse magistrates & officers among themselues to haue the power of transacting all the publique ciuill affayres of this Plantatio[n] . . . ." The River Colony never made church membership a requirement for civil voting. New Haven, however, created a theocracy, or church-state, in which a carefully regulated church membership completely dominated the political state. It appears that New Haven took as its guide a code of laws prepared by John Cotton called "Moses his judicials."

Not until October 25, 1639, did the seven pillars launch the civil government which they considered secondary to the religious one. They could select nine persons from approved churches as burgesses, thus increasing the electorate to the lofty total of sixteen!

Still uncertain of the colony's safety, the court required that each man must furnish himself with a sword, a bandoleer, a musket, powder and bullets. A guard was organized in June 1640 and later commanded by Captain Nathaniel Turner. Even on Sunday those on duty were expected to be completely armed and others to bring their swords.

The small New Haven Colony seemed to have everything in its favor—able leadership, a well-disciplined homogenous population, high morals and morale, a strong sense of purpose and much wealth. In 1643, for instance, ten people possessed an estate worth £1,000 or more. Eaton with £3,000 and 963 acres headed the list. Another twenty-seven men held substantial estates worth £400-£900. It is entirely possible that the New Haven group ranked first in wealth among all English groups settling in America before 1700.

The Five Children of New Haven

New Haven soon boasted a promising brood of children—five in all: Milford, Guilford, Branford, Stamford and Southold on Long Island. The first offspring was Milford—brainchild of Peter Prudden. While he and his followers worked harmoniously with others in New Haven, they never forgot their ardent aspirations to have a colony of their own. In the summer of 1638 Prudden preached in Wethersfield where he won many followers. In combination with his New Haven supporters he at last had enough manpower to plan a new settlement. In February 1638/39 representatives of the joint group concluded the purchase of land ten miles west of New Haven from Ansantawae, a sachem of the Paugusset Indians. Acquisition of this particular area, Wepowaug, stemmed from a recommendation by Sergeant Thomas Tibbals who had observed its attractiveness during the Pequot campaign.

In the fall of 1639 the Prudden group settled in Wepowaug,

soon renamed Milford. The town imitated New Haven in most respects even to choosing seven pillars. Prudden was the leading religious and intellectual figure in Milford's development until his death in 1656. Cotton Mather observed that Prudden "was noted for a singular faculty to sweeten, compose and qualify *exasperated spirits,* and stop or heal all contentions." While predominantly a farming community, Milford soon developed a prosperous coastal trade.

In time sentiment developed for a formal association with New Haven. Milford applied for membership in New Haven Colony but was rejected because it had enfranchised six nonchurch members. After much consultation the New Haven fathers agreed in 1643 to admit Milford if in the future it would admit only church members as freemen.

Guilford, the next addition to New Haven, also was very much the product of one man's inspiring leadership—that of Henry Whitfield. Son of a lawyer and educated at Oxford University, he obtained a church at Ockley, Surrey. Influenced by Cotton, Davenport and Hooker he became a strong Puritan. Gathering a group of fellow-Puritans from his native Surrey and adjoining Kent, in May 1639 he brought them on the first ship sailing directly from England to New Haven.

Soon after arrival the Whitfield group consummated a land purchase at Menunkatuck because its fertile soil and topography strongly resembled their native counties. As might be expected, Guilford became almost entirely a farming community.

As Whitfield and his wife had a large family on their arrival, they pushed the construction of a handsome house, which looked exactly like the home of an English country gentleman. This stone edifice, largely restored, and known as the "Old Stone House," still stands in Guilford and is claimed to be the oldest stone house in the United States.

Guilford's theocracy was the strictest of all the towns, requiring that only members of their own church could vote and a committee carefully screen membership applications. In 1643 the settlers chose Guilford as a permanent name, apparently to honor Guildford, Surrey. Whitfield himself seems to have been affluent, but most of his followers were of relatively humble circumstances.

In relatively quick order Branford, Stamford and Southold were founded. In 1644 a group of planters from Wethersfield, headed by William Swaine, accepted an invitation from New Haven to settle east of New Haven at Totoket. As pastor the settlers called the Reverend Abraham Pierson from Southampton, Long Island. The new town also modeled itself after New Haven and worked closely with it. In 1653 Totoket was renamed Branford, apparently after Brentford, Middlesex, near London.

In 1640 Captain Nathaniel Turner on behalf of New Haven purchased from Indians a tract about thirty-five miles westward called Rippowams, later named Stamford. To find settlers New Haven as usual turned to Wethersfield, again seething with internal strife. A faction headed by the Reverend Richard Denton accepted Davenport's invitation. They first agreed to acknowledge New Haven's rule, emulate its theocratic system and repay money expended for land. Then in the spring of 1641 Denton and about thirty families moved to their new homes.

The final New Haven outpost was established at Southold, Long Island—almost straight across the Sound. In 1640 New Haven bought the land from an agent of the Earl of Stirling who had been granted Long Island by the Council for New England. The first settlers in the area came from Salem, Massachusetts, under the leadership of the Reverend John Youngs.

Actually, in practice, the six New Haven-associated towns functioned independently until 1643. The founding of the New England Confederation that year forced New Haven and its five offshoots to consolidate as a single colony to procure its protection. In 1643 the six towns formally joined together as the New Haven Colony.

On October 17, 1643, the General Court adopted a fundamental order as a frame of government. Only members of approved churches were allowed to participate in the new government. Each October a General Court containing two deputies from each town was to choose a governor, deputy governor, secretary, treasurer and marshal. All applauded the choice of Eaton as the first governor. Although individual town courts continued to function, a new court of magistrates was established for major legal cases. None of the courts permitted trial by jury—in contrast to other New England colonies.

Need for Intercolonial Organization

As time passed the New England colonies developed serious. problems, accentuating the need for intercolonial cooperation. Some of the disputes between the English colonies had engendered bitter feelings and in the distance lurked the ominous shadows of the French and Dutch. Both the Dutch and English claimed large areas located between their settlements and the Dutch fort at Hartford irritated the English. As already noted, Windsor was born amidst conflicting claims of Plymouth and Massachusetts Bay. Massachusetts and Plymouth also disputed the line of their common boundary.

The initiative toward intercolonial organization came from Massachusetts which in 1638 proposed that each colony send two or more commissioners to a meeting authorized to draw up a plan of union. That summer the River Colony sent a delegation with proposed revisions. After a warm discussion, counterproposals were returned to Hartford. A sharp correspondence between Winthrop and Hooker ensued, producing a temporary impasse. Eventually the Indian menace, boundary disputes and the increasing French and Dutch threats, among other things, pushed the New England colonies toward common action.

After serious discussions at Boston in 1643 the delegates from Massachusetts Bay, Plymouth, the River Colony and New Haven adopted articles creating the New England Confederation. They provided for a defensive and offensive alliance aimed at preserving the safety and liberty of the four member colonies. The Confederation deliberately excluded Rhode Island, Maine and New Hampshire —areas of unorthodox Puritan views and potential targets for future acquisition by Massachusetts.

The Confederation left each member fully independent and in control of its territory. With two commissioners per colony it required six votes to pass a resolution. In theory, therefore, the three smaller colonies could outvote the Bay Colony. Each colony would contribute funds for common defense proportionate to the adult male population and send two commissioners to an annual meeting. The Confederation lacked the power to compel any colony or individual to abide by any resolution.

The Confederation started very inauspiciously. In 1643 a quarrel broke out between Uncas, Mohegan chief, and Sequassen, Saukiog chief. Governor Haynes and the Court tried in vain to mediate the dispute. Uncas and his warriors launched a sudden attack on Sequassen, killed some of his men and seized many spoils. This led Miantonomo, ally of Sequassen, to seek permission from the English for a retaliatory attack. Receiving sanction he attacked the Mohegans with about 1,000 warriors. Outnumbered over two to one, Uncas and his warriors won handily and captured Miantonomo. He was brought to Hartford and left in white custody while his fate was debated by the Confederation commissioners at Boston. They decided equivocally that it was neither prudent to release him nor proper to execute him. At this point the matter was referred to "five of the most judicious elders" of the Bay Colony who recommended death. The reasons cited by Winthrop for the sentence appear most inconsequential when compared with Miantonomo's valuable services to the English, especially during the Pequot War. So without anything resembling a legal trial he was unceremoniously handed over to Uncas who had him executed. The Confederation certainly had taken a cowardly and dishonorable course.

For over twenty years the Confederation devoted much attention to relations with the Dutch. Since the English colonies were growing far more rapidly than New Netherlands, time worked in their favor. The River Colony charged misconduct by the Dutch garrison at Good Hope. In reply Governor Kieft observed that "when we heare the inhabitants of Hartford complayninge of vs, we seeme to heare Esops wolfe complayninge of the lamb." The English and Dutch signed an agreement at Hartford in September 1650, but it proved no more than a truce.

In 1653 war almost broke out between the Confederation and the Dutch. Strong rumors arose that the Dutch and Indians intended to massacre all of the Connecticut colonists. Three meetings of the Confederation commissioners in April, May and September 1653 each produced a six-to-two vote in favor of war against the Dutch. Only Massachusetts opposed, but so adamantly that the other colonies hesitated to proceed. Both New Haven and the River Colony put heavy pressure on Massachusetts to comply with the majority viewpoint, but in vain. The ending of the first Anglo-

Dutch war in 1654 greatly eased fear of a Dutch attack against Connecticut. The River Colony in 1654 simply voted to dissolve the Dutch post and that conclusively terminated Dutch colonizing in Connecticut.

Hooker and His Legacy

Meanwhile Connecticut suffered a great loss. Early in the summer of 1647 an epidemic swept through sections of New England and claimed Thomas Hooker. The unquestioned leader of the River Colony, he influenced its early development enormously. His previous career in England, Holland and Massachusetts served primarily to prepare him for his final eleven years at Hartford—1636 to 1647—where he developed the Puritan state of which he had dreamed in old England.

Throughout his final decade Hooker retained close ties with Boston. In 1637 he returned in connection with Anne Hutchinson's trial. In 1639, in company with Haynes, he spent a month there, mostly on Confederation possibilities. In September 1643 he participated in the famous Cambridge Synod and returned in 1645 for a church council. The group approved Hooker's influential book, *A Survey of the Summe of Church-Discipline,* and sent it to England for printing. Unfortunately the manuscript was lost when the ship from New Haven sank. Hooker returned unhappily to his task, but death intervened before its conclusion. Friends forwarded it to London where it was printed in 1648. The *Survey* constituted what has been acclaimed "the supreme exposition of the Congregational church polity."

Actually Hooker published little else that attracted wide attention. His typical book consisted of a sermon, or sermons, apparently prepared for oral delivery and not revised for publication. In fact several were published posthumously. Hooker admitted, too, that he was not a polished writer:

> As it is beyond my skill, so I professe it is beyond my care to please the nicenesse of mens palates, with any quaintnesse of language. They who covet more sauce than meat, they must provide cooks to their minde.

In his sermons one reads not erudite theology but practical straightforward solutions to typical daily problems.

As pastor of Hartford's church Hooker enjoyed great success. In part, at least, this may be attributed to his unusual skill in dealing with people. When his congregation became embroiled in a dispute, he had the matter tabled. Prior to the next meeting he "would ordinarily by private conferences, gain over such as were unsatisfied." Before a major issue was presented to the congregation he often consulted the leading elders and won their support. In applications for membership he required that the elders conduct the necessary examination. Thus by painstaking groundwork and close attention to the wishes of the members he obtained an atmosphere of genuine brotherly love in his church. During his entire Hartford pastorate only one member was censured and one excommunicated.

Grouped with Cotton and Davenport in the triumvirate of leading Puritan theocrats in New England, Hooker clearly ranks as the most liberal of the three. He advocated a larger role for the individual church member as well as the congregation. He emphasized man as a rational creature and minimized him as a miserable sinner. Always an ardent Puritan and firm believer in strong pastoral leadership, he gave the River Colony a more democratic church than Massachusetts knew. He meant his 1638 statement that the covenant was built on "the free consent of the people." Men were free to join in a fellowship of faith and free to leave. Yet the church members "must give way while he [the minister] delivers the mind of Christ out of the Gospel, and acts all the affairs of his Kingdome, according to his rule; and as it suits with his mind."

In the modern usage of the word "democrat" Hooker fails to qualify. By declaring that authority originated from *below* rather than *above* he anticipated the theory of popular sovereignty. Unlike Cotton and Winthrop he believed that eventually all men could attain full religious and civil rights. When one compares him with such New England radicals as Roger Williams and Anne Hutchinson, he appears very conservative. Yet for his Puritan age he must be placed well over on the "liberal" side. When one considers the broad range of his contributions as minister, preacher, theologian, author, colonizer, mediator and shaper of the Fundamental Orders, he richly deserves a place among the greatest leaders of seventeenth-century America.

References Consulted

Charles M. Andrews, *The Colonial Period of American History*, II (New Haven, 1936)

——, *The Rise and Fall of the New Haven Colony*, Connecticut Tercentenary Commission Publications, No. 48 (New Haven, 1936)

——, *The River Towns of Connecticut* (Baltimore, 1889)

Howard Bradstreet, *The Story of the War with the Pequots Re-Told*, Connecticut Tercentenary Commission Publications, No. 5 (New Haven, 1933)

Isabel M. Calder, *The New Haven Colony* (New Haven, 1934)

Charles J. Hoadly, *The Warwick Patent* (Hartford, 1902)

John Mason, *Brief History of the Pequot War* . . .(Boston, 1736)

Rollin G. Osterweis, *Three Centuries of New Haven, 1638-1938* (New Haven, 1953)

Henry R. Stiles, *The History and Genealogies of Ancient Windsor, Connecticut* . . . (Hartford, 1891)

——, *The History of Ancient Wethersfield, Connecticut* . . . (New York, 1904)

Benjamin Trumbull, *A Complete History of Connecticut* . . . (New London, 1898)

J. Hammond Trumbull, ed., *The Public Records of the Colony of Connecticut* . . . I (Hartford, 1850)

George L. Walker, *Thomas Hooker: Preacher, Founder, Democrat* (New York, 1891)

Harry M. Ward, *The United Colonies of New England—1643-90* (New York, Washington, Hollywood, 1961)

IV A New Charter and Resulting Boundary Disputes

John Winthrop, Jr., Emerges as a Dynamic Leader

John Winthrop, Jr., (1606-76) was one of the towering figures of seventeenth-century America. A man of amazingly diversified interests, he left England for Massachusetts, and later Massachusetts for Connecticut. So influential was his career that it is worth recounting its highlights before considering his mission to secure Connecticut's charter.

Born in Groton, Suffolk, England, in 1606 of a solid country gentry family, he grew up amidst the beautiful gently rolling countryside of Suffolk. His father, later the famous governor of Massachusetts Bay, became a stanch Puritan about 1606. While considered a Puritan, too, the son never became a really devout one. The recipient of an excellent training at the King Edward VI School in Bury St. Edmunds, Winthrop attended Trinity College, Dublin—an institution of liberal outlook. Unfortunately he found Trinity uncongenial and dropped out. Later he studied law at the Inner Temple in London, but again failed to graduate. Still very immature, he suddenly grew up under the impact of two experiences at sea—one, participation in the unsuccessful siege of La Rochelle, France; and two, a voyage to Constantinople and Venice.

Through his father's influence, young Winthrop became involved in the Massachusetts Bay Company's affairs and in 1631 decided to follow his father to Boston where he was soon made an assistant. In 1633, however, he left and founded Ipswich where he lived only briefly. Returning to England, he became involved in the colonizing schemes of the Earl of Warwick and his friends. As already noted, in 1635 Winthrop accepted their commission as governor of Saybrook Colony which in 1636 he irresponsibly deserted. Until this time his career seemed only a series of enthusiastic beginnings to ambitious projects—each suddenly abandoned.

In 1641 Winthrop returned to England, then traveled on the Continent where he met a number of leading intellectuals. Back in England he raised capital and secured men and equipment for an ironmaking enterprise in Massachusetts. After setting up the works at Braintree, he characteristically departed.

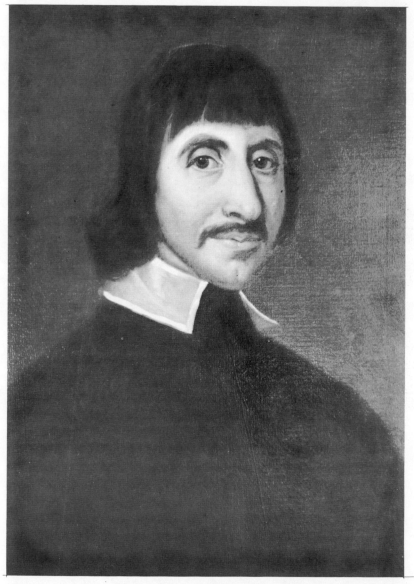

Courtesy of Connecticut State Library. Photo by Clarence Casabella

John Winthrop, Jr. (1606-76).

His next venture in 1646 was the establishment of a colony called Pequot near the mouth of the Thames River in Connecticut. When Connecticut claims to the colony prevailed over those of Massachusetts, Winthrop's future became entwined with Connecticut. Pequot did its best to keep the magnetic Winthrop as a permanent resident by granting him all that his heart could desire—a great sandy beach to use in glassmaking, a ferry monopoly, all the islands of rocks within the harbors, a mill privilege, quarrying rights and tax-free land. In truth, Winthrop came close to being the lord of Pequot (later renamed New London). Like most new colonies New London experienced such difficulties that prosperity eluded it. In 1651 Connecticut voters elected him an assistant. Finally, and almost accidentally, he began developing genuine roots in Connecticut.

As always, other communities implored the talented and personable Winthrop to settle among them. Roger Williams invited him to Providence, but New Haven's lure proved more compelling as it offered a fine free residence, and even a good maidservant. New Haven wanted Winthrop for his sense of enterprise, entrepreneurial skills (ironmaking), personality, prestige and medical skills. Perhaps moved most by the presence of bogs and other potential for ironmaking, Winthrop left a shocked New London in 1656 and moved to New Haven. Just as he was settling down there, the River Colony chose him governor in 1657. This stroke of political genius snatched Winthrop from rival New Haven and gave Connecticut an able leader. Winthrop occupied an official residence in Hartford part of each year but remained a legal resident of New London.

Such was Winthrop's great popularity in the River Colony that the provision of the Fundamental Orders prohibiting the governor from being elected two years in a row was repealed in 1660. Winthrop then received the honor of re-election annually until his death in 1676.

He performed gubernatorial duties with general satisfaction and found time also to continue his varied personal interests, including a large medical practice. Robert C. Black, author of a fascinating biography of Winthrop, reports that in the years from 1657-69 Winthrop treated at least 700 different individuals! He kept abreast of the activities of Europe's intellectuals through correspondence with several Europeans, including Samuel Hartlib of London, a patron of scholars.

England's Puritan rule ended abruptly in 1660 with the Stuart restoration of Charles II to the throne. Many confirmed enemies of Puritan New England moved into positions of power in London. Connecticut having no official charter lacked legitimacy in official eyes.

Winthrop's Charter Mission

After three decades of happy experience under the Fundamental Orders, in 1660 Connecticut suddenly realized that the fall of Cromwell's Puritan government also had destroyed Connecticut's security. In English eyes the colony possessed no legal basis. Connecticut's leaders, and especially Winthrop, realized that they must take positive action. On March 14, 1660/61, the legislature voted to prepare an address to the King and petition him for a confirmation of the privileges requisite for "the comfortable and peaceable settlement" of Connecticut. In other words, they desired a charter. The legislature appointed Governor Winthrop, Deputy Governor John Mason and seven others to prepare the petition and letters to certain "noble p[e]rsonages" who might prove helpful.

For the delicate mission to London the legislators selected the most personable and popular man in Connecticut—Governor Winthrop. He was given complete flexibility in how he proceeded to achieve his goal.

The first obstacle to success was the New Haven Colony's desire to preserve its separate existence. Aware of the threatening mien of Charles II's government, Davenport and many other New Haveners wanted security for their colony, but not at the cost of absorption into Connecticut. Governor Leete, however, leaned toward some sort of federal union with Connecticut. He visited Hartford to confer with Winthrop, but no firm agreement was reached. When Davenport wrote on June 16, 1661, asking Winthrop to delay his trip at least one year, Winthrop carefully refrained from answering until he had departed! Winthrop also deliberately avoided consultations with the other New England colonies who were worried about their relationship to the new English government.

52

By July 5, 1661, Winthrop had quietly left Hartford, bypassed New Haven and sailed to New Amsterdam. Poor Governor Leete must have raged as he looked at his petition specifically prepared for Winthrop to carry to the King!

After a tedious journey on a Dutch boat to Holland, Winthrop at last reached London on September 18. He found quarters at the home of William Whiting on Coleman Street, next door to Davenport's old church. Winthrop and Connecticut possessed some powerful friends including Lord Say and Sele (unfortunately away and very feeble); Lord Brooke, also a Warwick patentee; and the Earl of Manchester, then Lord Chamberlain of the Household. As it developed, Winthrop's close friend, Samuel Hartlib, proved more valuable than any of these. He informed Winthrop that he could achieve nothing at Court without a powerful go-between. Hartlib suggested cultivating Benjamin Worsley who had the confidence of the Lord Chancellor on most colonial affairs. Winthrop almost immediately began this ingratiating process with Worsley. As with all official matters, however, many weeks were required for the tedious charter-acquiring process.

Letters arrived from Leete and Plymouth Colony asking his assistance in obtaining royal assent to their petitions. Technically Winthrop honored their requests by filing these petitions as requested, but there is no evidence that he really worked for either colony.

As a sophisticated and worldly Puritan, Winthrop enthusiastically savored the delights of London. Through introductions from Hartlib he met many of the leading savants of England. He found particularly congenial William Brereton who had affiliated with a notable group of intellectuals calling themselves "The Royal Society." Winthrop was delighted with this eminent group who fully reciprocated. On January 1, 1661/62, they voted to make him a member—the first North American admitted. That year he delivered papers on three New England topics: making tar and pitch, shipbuilding and Indian corn and its uses. Reflective of another longtime interest, Winthrop, through the assistance of Worsley, procured a good astronomical telescope much superior to the one he had previously used.

Meanwhile negotiations slowly moved forward through tortuous official channels. Winthrop never found the original Warwick Patent—a document he had hoped would establish Connecticut's land claims. Then he discovered that Connecticut's petition failed to meet court standards. So he rewrote it twice. Probably on February 12, 1661/62, he personally presented Connecticut's revised petition to the King in council. Couching his case in felicitous phraseology, he made such a fine impression that the whole process was greatly expedited. The final engrossment and passage of the great seal occurred on May 10, 1662. Winthrop had won the greatest victory of his career!

There was little opportunity to enjoy his triumph as a serious dispute developed immediately with Dr. John Clarke who was seeking a charter for Rhode Island. He asked for a review of the Connecticut charter because it seemed to trespass on Rhode Island's claims. This caused a long delay in Winthrop's departure though fortunately he sent off a copy of the charter to Connecticut. After months of delay English arbitrators placed the Connecticut-Rhode Island boundary at the Pawcatuck River and temporarily settled other issues. At long last Winthrop took his final leave of London and reached Connecticut in June 1663.

An Amazing Charter

Connecticut's charter of 1662 was so generous as to be almost unbelievable. The King not only gave Connecticut a clear legal title, but also a surprising amount of self-government. The charter constituted John Winthrop, Jr., and others a body corporate entitled the "Governour and Company of the English Colony of Conecticut in New England in America." The company members were freemen with full powers of a corporation. The charter called for a governor, deputy governor and twelve assistants to be elected annually in May by the freemen. Twice yearly this upper house met with a lower house of two members per town to conduct the colony's business as the General Assembly. The freemen holding all the "liberties and Immunities" of natural-born Englishmen must take the oath of supremacy. The legislature or the governor or deputy governor and six assistants would exercise full judicial powers. The legislature could enact laws as long as none contravened those of England.

54

The freemen received the freest type of land tenure in England —that of the Manor of East Greenwich. In recompense, the Crown was granted one-fifth of all gold and silver mined in Connecticut. As it turned out, there was none!

The charter fixed remarkable boundaries: Narragansett Bay on the east; Massachusetts on the north; Long Island Sound and the Atlantic Ocean on the south; and the "South Sea," meaning the Pacific Ocean, on the west! This generous grant precipitated lengthy and stubborn boundary disputes with Rhode Island, Massachusetts, New York and Pennsylvania. Even so, this charter which would serve Connecticut, with modifications, for 156 years, marks Winthrop's greatest single achievement. Only a person possessing consummate skill in politics could have engineered so striking a triumph!

New Haven Fights Connecticut

Well before Winthrop returned to Connecticut, the authorities at Hartford informed New Haven leaders that the new charter meant annexation of New Haven Colony. On March 20, 1662/63, a Connecticut committee presented to New Haven magistrates a detailed and reasonable proposal for union—which New Haven rejected. Public opinion in New Haven was divided with the Davenport-Nicholas Street faction intransigent in its opposition, and the Leete faction willing to accept a face-saving solution involving union. Even so, Leete warned Hartford of likely "violent fomentations" in New Haven. On his return Winthrop played for time and hoped that tensions would subside. In view of New Haven's declining economic and political condition, Winthrop's delaying tactics made sense.

Meanwhile, Connecticut faced possible serious objection from the New England Confederation whose articles guaranteed the integrity of each member. New Haven filed complaints against Connecticut and they were aired. Winthrop replied in masterful fashion and largely defused the opposition. Definite action was postponed with a statement expressing hope for an amicable settlement.

Connecticut's assembly appointed a committee to negotiate. It offered New Haven generous terms: a proportionate number of assistants, full status for New Haven freemen as Connecticut free-

55

men, no interference with their churches and two deputies for each New Haven Colony town. New Haven rejected these. The conservative faction construed union as the victory of the less orthodox political and religious establishment in Connecticut—a prospect so terrifying as to lead some to consider migration to New Netherlands!

As Winthrop so astutely reasoned, time was playing into Connecticut's hands. Within a short period Southold, Stamford and Greenwich deserted New Haven for Connecticut, while Guilford threatened to leave. Only Branford and Milford remained loyal through 1662 and 1663. Early in 1664 New Haven's Court authorized Davenport and Street to write a paper stating the colony's arguments. Their effort resulted in "Newhavens Case Stated," a vigorous assault on Connecticut's encroachments. Connecticut responded that it possessed a new charter calling for union and had made a generous offer.

The possibility of English interference worried both sides. A special royal commission appointed in April 1664 to study conditions in New England posed a threat to all colonies there. Massachusetts advised Connecticut to effect an agreement with New Haven before all New England charters were rescinded. Connecticut promptly forwarded this practical advice to New Haven and recommended acceptance of union.

In New Haven, meanwhile, the situation was steadily deteriorating. The treasury was nearly exhausted and the colony was disintegrating. That same year a dramatic event occurred in New Amsterdam when Director General Peter Stuyvesant surrendered his colony to an English force. Anticipating this conquest, Charles II in March 1664 had already granted this colony, with boundaries extending eastward to the Connecticut River, to the Duke of York. Faced with a choice between rule by Winthrop or James Stuart (Duke of York), even the most recalcitrant New Haveners preferred Winthrop!

The unpleasant dispute then moved swiftly to its climax, but with concern shown for New Haven's feelings. In September a Confederation meeting at Hartford urged final settlement and consented to the union. In October the Connecticut assembly voted to send a delegation to New Haven requiring submission of all New

Haven Colony inhabitants and making their freemen also freemen of Connecticut. In addition, the assembly appointed seven New Haven leaders as magistrates to act in a liaison capacity for New Haven. In November Milford recognized the inevitable by voting to join Connecticut. Late that month after discussions with Winthrop and others royal commissioners decided that Long Island belonged to New York and Connecticut's western and southern boundary lay at Mamaroneck River and Long Island Sound respectively. This confirmed Connecticut's claim to the New Haven Colony. In December, therefore, New Haven's General Court reluctantly voted submission to Connecticut with the formal act passing on January 5, 1664/65. Two days later New Haven's cause finally died when the town of New Haven capitulated! Characteristically Winthrop took the occasion to write words of praise to Leete and comfort to Davenport.

For some New Haven die-hards emigration seemed preferable to rule by Connecticut. A group from Branford, Guilford, Milford and New Haven under Abraham Pierson in 1666 migrated to New Jersey and founded Milford, later called Newark.

John Davenport also remained bitterly unconsolable, and considered an invitation from Boston's First Church in 1667. Unhappily a strong minority there opposed him as too old and conservative. New Haven, still deeply devoted to its pastor, tried vainly to keep him. Yet, in November 1668, under ambiguous conditions Davenport finally accepted the Boston call. His ministry there produced secession by his opponents and much general turmoil. After a brief unhappy pastorate Davenport died in March 1669/70—an unhappy end for a man who had made such great contributions to New Haven.

Occasionally one finds a nostalgic statement that New Haven Colony might have retained its separateness and eventually become a state of the new United States. Perhaps there is some romantic appeal to this idea, but little else. For various reasons—no great river or large prosperous hinterland, inept commercial leadership and plain bad luck—the colony never prospered. Settling the boundaries of Connecticut and New York destroyed all hopes of future territorial expansion. Internally, too, discontent grew over the ultraconservative policies concerning church membership and political rights. Governor Leete served as spokesman for the more liberal group willing to reach an accommodation with Connecticut. In the final analysis the lack of a charter rendered New Haven helpless before her larger neighbor, Connecticut, recently legitimized by the charter of 1662.

For the long-range success of the expanded Connecticut, capitulation by New Haven was an absolutely necessary, if painful, step forward. Only by the union of the two colonies could there be created a colony large enough to play an influential role in intercolonial and national affairs. It is regrettable that some Connecticut partisans pushed the merger so aggressively. The actual union, however, became effective surprisingly smoothly with New Haven contributing an able corps of leaders to the enlarged Connecticut. In 1669 William Leete, the last governor of New Haven, was elected deputy governor and in 1676 on Winthrop's death succeeded him as governor—a position he held until his passing in 1683. Furthermore, in May 1701 the assembly voted that henceforth the regular session in October should be held in New Haven, making it thereby a joint capital with Hartford.

Connecticut's Battle to Defend and Expand Its Boundaries

The charter of 1662 contained ambiguities which produced a series of sharp disagreements with Connecticut's neighbors. In fact, boundary disputes even antedated the charter.

The earliest conflict to develop—that with Massachusetts—centered on the location of Connecticut's northern boundary. The Massachusetts charter provided that its southern boundary should run due west from a line three miles south of the southernmost part of the Charles River. In 1642 Massachusetts engaged Nathaniel Woodward and Solomon Saffery to survey this line. After commencing the survey apparently at the correct location they decided that it was too much trouble to extend it on foot, so they sailed around Cape Cod and up the Connecticut River to a point which they *thought* to be on the same latitude as their beginning point! In reality this new point lay eight miles farther south. As a result, the Woodward-Saffery line, as it stretched eastward, neatly cut an illegal piece out of Connecticut—eight miles broad at the widest, and four miles at the narrowest.

58

Irritated by this serious discrepancy, Connecticut eventually ordered its own survey which John Butcher and William Whiting finished in 1695. Connecticut settlers meanwhile had established homes in Enfield and Suffield—an area claimed by both colonies. In 1702 the two colonies arranged a new joint survey which returned most of the disputed land to Connecticut. Then Massachusetts reneged on the agreement and in 1708 each colony dispatched a vigorous petition to London.

At that time, however, much feeling existed in English official circles favoring revocation of all private colonial charters. The New Englanders realized that it might be diplomatic to adjust their boundary conflict before London imposed some drastic solution. In 1713, therefore, they reached an agreement which left Massachusetts in control of Enfield, Suffield and Woodstock while yielding land elsewhere to Connecticut. In 1716 Connecticut sold this noncontiguous land for £683 and allocated the money to hard-pressed Yale College.

The new line, however, cavalierly ignored the real wishes of Enfield, Suffield and Woodstock. Moved particularly by Massachusetts' higher taxes, in 1724 they openly petitioned Connecticut to admit them. Rebuffed in this, they renewed the attempt in 1747. Moving gingerly in this complicated matter, Connecticut finally in 1749 voted to take Enfield, Somers, Suffield and Woodstock; appointed commissioners to negotiate with Massachusetts; and threatened an appeal to Britain. To heighten the crisis Woodstock even elected deputies to the Connecticut legislature! Britain ignored the matter and Connecticut continued to govern the four towns. By 1800 Massachusetts had ceased to challenge the *de facto* situation.

After 1800 the two states settled three minor boundary disputes. The claims of Southwick, Massachusetts, to parts of Granby and Suffield were adjusted by giving a small segment of Granby to Massachusetts. This created the only jog in the otherwise straight northern boundary from the Connecticut River westward. Minor adjustments farther east were made, also, and in May 1827 when Connecticut accepted these changes peace reigned on the Massachusetts-Connecticut boundary after 185 years of contention.

The battle between Connecticut and Rhode Island, while shorter in duration, proved more important. In fact, much of Rhode Is-

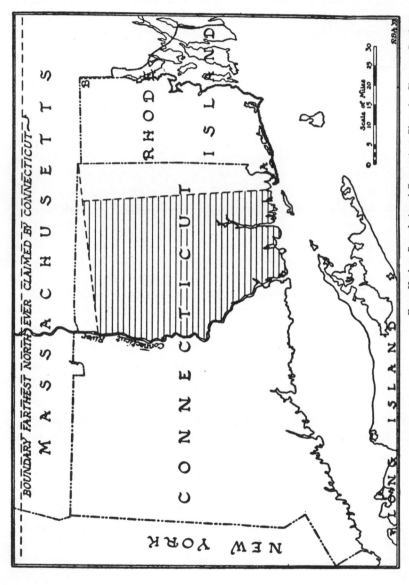

From Hooker, *Boundaries of Connecticut.* Photo by Clarence Casabella

What Connecticut might have been (shaded area) if all rival claims had prevailed.

land was at stake since the Connecticut charter set the eastern boundary at Narragansett Bay! As has already been seen, while Winthrop was still in London, Dr. John Clarke was seeking a charter for Rhode Island. The two men conferred and effected a tentative agreement on the Rhode Island-Connecticut line. This established the boundary at the Pawcatuck River with Winthrop renouncing all land east of it.

Unfortunately the Connecticut legislature repudiated this agreement. Royal commissioners attempted to negotiate in 1665, but to no avail. A stormy Connecticut-Rhode Island conference at New London in 1670 achieved nothing. Various unpleasant incidents in the disputed area culminated in 1680 with the arrest by Rhode Island of Stephen Richardson, a Connecticut constable exercising his authority at Westerly. Angered by Rhode Island's refusal to free him, Connecticut seized Joseph Clarke of Westerly, a Rhode Island partisan. In 1683 royal commissioners appointed by Charles II granted all the disputed Narragansett area to Connecticut, but due to lack of action by the Privy Council, the decision was never put into effect.

Later efforts by Edmund Andros and by New York's governor, the Earl of Bellomont, to mediate failed. When a Rhode Island sheriff and four assistants tried to seize Stonington property for nonpayment of taxes, they were arrested and fined by a Connecticut court.

Fearful of English revocation of their charters the contestants in 1703 agreed on a boundary along the Pawcatuck River and northward. When the survey was done in 1714, however, the agreement evaporated. In 1720 a disgusted Board of Trade, irritated by sixty years of wrangling in the case, recommended that both colonies lose their charters and be annexed to New Hampshire. This shock therapy worked wonders! The two colonies immediately promised to accept in advance any final ruling of the Privy Council whereupon the New Hampshire recommendation was rescinded. The Board of Trade then proposed a new line close to that set by the 1703 accord. A survey in 1728 made this official. The two colonies exchanged more unpleasantries but finally in 1742 accepted the boundary.

For Connecticut the boundary quarrel with New York posed

a far greater threat. This dispute grew out of Charles II's grant to his brother, James, Duke of York, of all the land from the Connecticut River to Delaware Bay. If implemented, this would have reduced Connecticut to a narrow corridor east of the Connecticut River. By an agreement in 1664 Connecticut achieved a generous line running across the Hudson at Peekskill and ending twenty-five miles west of the river. Unfortunately, the 1664 agreement never received royal confirmation. In May 1675 Andros, as governor of New York, called for Connecticut's surrender of all land west of the Connecticut River. Connecticut angrily rejected this demand. In July 1675 Andros suddenly arrived at Saybrook, presumably to press his claims. Captain Thomas Bull and two Connecticut militia companies discouraged him from further aggression. In 1683 after Thomas Dongan became New York governor, the two colonies accepted a line which generally ran twenty miles east of and parallel to the Hudson.

This agreement sacrificed Rye whose inhabitants since 1665 had considered themselves in Connecticut. Strongly preferring the greater local autonomy and lower taxes of Connecticut, Rye openly revolted in 1697 and joined Connecticut, as did nearby Bedford. In 1700 the King confirmed the 1683 agreement which placed Rye and Bedford in New York, where they stayed. Many years of verbal bickering between the states followed, and New Yorkers were confirmed in their suspicions of Connecticut as a land of "sharp traders." Connecticut, in turn, charged New York with having an autocratic government. Despite mutual suspicions the two governments negotiated an agreement in 1725. The resulting joint survey, finished in 1731, amazingly enough was accepted by both sides.

In 1855 the states agreed to resurvey the 1731 line since the markers had vanished and inhabitants along the boundary paid no taxes to either state. After much more wrangling Connecticut in 1880 accepted the resurveyed 1731 line in return for extension of its southern boundary into the Sound. In 1881 both states and Congress ratified the agreement and after over 200 years *all* of Connecticut's boundaries were finally fixed officially!

References Consulted

Charles M. Andrews, *The Beginnings of Connecticut, 1632-1662,* Connecticut Tercentenary Commission Publications, No. 32 (New Haven, 1934)

Albert C. Bates, *The Charter of Connecticut* . . . (Hartford, 1932)

Robert C. Black, III, *The Younger John Winthrop* (New York, London, 1966)

Clarence W. Bowen, *The Boundary Disputes of Connecticut* (Boston, 1882)

Isabel M. Calder, *The New Haven Colony* (New Haven, 1934)

Dixon R. Fox, *Yankees and Yorkers* (New York, 1940)

Roland M. Hooker, *Boundaries of Connecticut,* Connecticut Tercentenary Commission Publications, No. 11 (New Haven, 1933)

Rollin G. Osterweis, *Three Centuries of New Haven, 1638-1938* (New Haven, 1953)

J. Hammond Trumbull, ed., *The Public Records of the Colony of Connecticut* . . . II, III (Hartford, 1852, 1859)

V Relations with Indians and Andros

Uncertain and Troubled Indian Relations

With the signing in September 1638 of the agreement concerning the Pequots, they had ceased to exist as an independent tribe. Even so Indian-white relations in all of New England remained unstable for several decades. As already seen, strong fear of Indian uprisings insured organization of the New England Confederation in 1643. Soon hostility between the Mohegans and the Narragansets threatened to precipitate a general war. In 1645 the Confederation's commissioners decided that the Narragansets were the aggressors and they would reinforce Uncas. Connecticut's quota was forty men; New Haven's, thirty. Fortunately, before serious fighting developed the Narragansets and their allies, the Niantics, backed down, agreed to pay an indemnity, return Mohegan captives and give hostages to the Confederation. In the late 1640's and early 1650's Ninigret, Niantic leader, appeared before the Confederation to defend his tribe against assorted charges, including trying to resurrect the Pequot tribe. In 1654 the Confederation, outraged by Ninigret's constant violations of agreements, raised an army of over 300 men to coerce him into obedience.

Intransigent as Ninigret was, Uncas caused even more trouble. At various times he instigated raids against Narragansets, Niantics, Nipmucks and Pocumtucks. To reduce the dangers from wars the various colonies attempted to cut off supplies of arms and ammunition to natives. At the very first recorded meeting on April 26, 1636, the little court for the three river towns ordered that nobody trade arms or ammunition with Indians—the first of a series of similar enactments. On the theory that alcohol, powder and Indians did not mix well, later courts also prohibited sale of alcoholic beverages to Indians. Illustrative is the act of 1654 which noted much drunkenness prevailing among Indians to the great hazard of both themselves and the English. Hence the court declared the sale, barter or gift to an Indian of any wine, liquors, beer, cider or metheglin unlawful, under penalty of £5 for every pint.

In examining the broad range of relationships with Indians one commonly finds a negative attitude toward them. Yet this stereotype was far from being accurate. For example, Indians willing to abide by colonial laws and government could be accepted as inhabitants. Alden Vaughan's penetrating study of Indians and Puritans concludes that the Puritans are entitled to "a more favorable judgment" than has generally been granted. He believes, for example, that Indians usually received just treatment in Puritan courts. He and other authors have described the rather extensive missionary efforts among them. While one may argue about the effectiveness of the missionaries, the very fact of this activity revealed a genuine concern for their welfare. While the Code of 1650 listed many restrictions against Indians, it also requested Thomas Stanton, who spoke Indian languages, to go among the Indians twice yearly and instruct them in religion.

The Reverend John Eliot of Roxbury, Massachusetts, translated the Bible for the Indians in the early 1650's. Certain that this translation would be incomprehensible to Connecticut Indians, the Reverend Abraham Pierson of Branford, aided by Thomas Stanton, slowly and painfully prepared a bilingual catechism hopefully suited to Connecticut Algonkin tongues. Pierson preached among some Connecticut River tribes and remained active in missionary work until his departure to New Jersey in the mid-1660's.

Very prominent also in missionary work was the Reverend James Fitch of Norwich who commenced preaching to the Mohegans in 1671. He found his greatest obstacle in Uncas whom he described as an old wicked drunkard and "very vitious." Despite this, Fitch claimed thirty converts by 1674. In other areas little progress was made. Overall Connecticut carried on considerably less missionary activity than Massachusetts, but more than Rhode Island.

King Philip's War Breaks Out

At the best the total of Indian converts in New England was much too small to influence the gradual worsening of relations. In Massachusetts, especially, much suspicion existed between Indians and whites—a feeling which increased after the death in 1662 of Massasoit, sachem of Wampanoags and a trusted friend. Plymouth adopted a tough attitude toward Philip, new sachem, and tried to disarm his tribe. The Indians generally had acquired guns and later would use them effectively.

After major scares in 1667, 1669 and 1671, King Philip's War broke out in June 1675 at Swansea, Massachusetts, where several whites were slain. The outbreak apparently stemmed from the conviction and hanging of three Indians for murder of a Christian Indian. It began as a local struggle between the Wampanoags and two colonies—Massachusetts and Plymouth. Attempts to keep the Narragansets neutral failed, and subsequently many Indian tribes joined a loose alliance led by Philip and Canonchet, of the Narragansets.

Connecticut reacted cautiously to the new conflict, and took no offensive measures until July 1, 1675, when alarms from New London and Stonington resulted in an order to dispatch forty men to those towns. In July the assembly created a special council to meet any emergencies arising between regular assembly meetings. Fortunately Connecticut was in little danger since it was located far from the fighting area and protected by the firm alliance with Uncas who could be counted on to oppose his old enemies, the Narragansets.

In August 1675 Brookfield, Massachusetts, was attacked and Springfield felt threatened. With the upper Connecticut River Valley erupting, the Connecticut council considered the war as coming much too close for comfort. They, therefore, made Major Robert Treat commander of Connecticut troops, a position he held for the war's duration. After the Pocumtuck Indians burned Deerfield, Connecticut took precautionary steps, such as night watches in all towns. Frightened by further attacks in the upper valley, the Confederation voted to increase the authorized total to 1,000 men, of which Connecticut's quota was 315. Despite this move the Indians raided Springfield, destroying thirty houses. Rumors of impending attacks on Connecticut multiplied.

Despite the spread of the war the Narragansets had remained neutral. When they refused to give up the Wampanoag refugees, however, the Confederation declared war against them. In December troops from three colonies, including 300 whites and 150 Indians from Connecticut, joined in Rhode Island for a showdown with the Narragansets who had fortified a village on a hillock in a cedar swamp. After a bitter encounter with heavy losses, the wigwams caught fire and a great massacre of Narragansets resulted. The hor-

66

ror of the affair was heightened by the subsequent eighteen-mile march through deep snow to Wickford. Some forty Connecticut men were killed or expired from the battle and exposure on the march, and as many were wounded.

While the Narragansets suffered a great defeat, they and their allies continued the war. Meanwhile plans for a new colonial offensive met resistance in Connecticut because of the recent heavy casualties in Rhode Island. On March 9 Philip, Canonchet and the Pocumtuck and Nipmuck chiefs held a council near Northfield and vowed to win a decisive victory, while their women and children raised crops and fished undisturbed in the deserted Connecticut Valley between Deerfield and Northfield.

At first the Indians enjoyed great success as raiding parties hit such towns as Concord, Lancaster, Springfield, Northampton, Medford, Groton, Weymouth and Marlborough. Even Providence seemed in dire danger though Roger Williams himself was trusted by the Indians. A small band of Indians invaded Connecticut, killed Henry Denslow at Windsor Locks (then Pine Meadow) and looted and burned the empty houses of Simsbury. Further grief afflicted the colony when word arrived of the death at Boston of Governor Winthrop—undoubtedly Connecticut's most cherished leader since Thomas Hooker.

While the winter and early spring of 1676 had brought a great surge of Indian victories, the momentum suddenly ran out. In April some Connecticut volunteers, aided by Indians, captured Canonchet near Pawcatuck River. His execution by other Indians removed one of the most audacious war leaders. A joint Massachusetts-Connecticut expedition in June cleared the valley of Indians in the Hadley area. Another raid through the Narraganset country inflicted sizable casualties. The incessant white attacks gradually destroyed the Indian food supplies and shattered the Indian alliance.

The Indians, no longer able to raise enough food to maintain themselves and fight a war, began to crumble. During July a Plymouth pardon offer resulted in surrender of over 300 Indians. King Philip himself was killed by an Indian ally in a Rhode Island swamp.

In late July Connecticut troops under Major John Talcott pushed their last campaign against a remnant of about 250 Indians fleeing westward. On August 15, 1676, near Great Barrington, Connecticut troops trapped their prey. In a battle of attempted encirclement the troops killed thirty-five and captured twenty, while the others escaped. This completed Connecticut's active fighting in the war.

It had been an extremely costly war for both sides. Massachusetts had many towns destroyed and 2,000 people left temporarily dependent on public relief. The Indians suffered far greater losses in death and privation. Many were bound over as servants to colonists to aid in rebuilding ruined towns. Plymouth even sold many captives into slavery.

In comparison, Connecticut's Indian policy was more humane. The assembly voted that all hostile Indians surrendering by January 1676/77 should not be sold as slaves, but be held in service for ten years after which they should live peacefully in their respective towns. The Reverend James Fitch, of Norwich, ever a friend to Indians, fought against allowing Uncas to care for Indian prisoners. As a result the governor and council resettled the Indians under white supervision.

While Connecticut's losses were only a fraction of those of Massachusetts Bay and Plymouth, the war cost heavily in men and money. For substantial periods one-seventh of the militia saw active service. Taxes rose from one penny on the pound in May 1674 to eighteen pence in October 1676. Fortunately, no town except Simsbury was damaged. Moreover the Indians within Connecticut helped the whites so not one Connecticut unit ever was ambushed. For New England as a whole it was fortunate that the last, great, internal Indian challenge was decisively defeated before the outbreak of French-English intercolonial struggles.

Growing Threats to Connecticut's Independence

Much more deeply threatening to Connecticut than the Indians was the danger coming from New York. In 1674 the Duke of York appointed as governor Major Edmund Andros, an English soldier and aristocrat. That same year the Duke of York obtained a new charter from Charles II giving him all land from the Connecticut River to the Delaware River. In 1675 Andros sought to implement this grant by demanding surrender of all land west of the Connecticut River. To reinforce his words on July 8, 1675, Andros suddenly besieged Saybrook with armed sloops. The assembly strongly denounced this invasion, and authorized resistance. Captain Thomas Bull, unintimidated, mustered his men in battle formation. The next morning Andros came ashore to confer with him. Seeing that a bloody battle might erupt, Andros prudently sailed away.

While the New York threat faded away, new dangers were developing in London. Some English leaders felt that it would be economically and politically advantageous to unite all New England colonies under one royal government. Such a government could encourage greater production of keenly desired English products—naval stores, hemp, minerals and raw materials. In turn New England could purchase more English manufactured goods. Furthermore, the increasing French power in America suggested the need of integrating defense efforts in New England. The investigations of Edward Randolph in Massachusetts had revealed flagrant violations of the Navigation Acts and other laws. Under a writ issued in 1685, Connecticut also was charged with passing laws contrary to English ones, enforcing a Connecticut oath of fidelity, denying freedom of worship and ignoring the oath of supremacy and allegiance.

Randolph returned to New England in May 1686 and informed Governor Treat that he held two writs against Connecticut under which the King intended to unite New England under one goverment and expected Connecticut's "humble submission."

Andros Tries to Rule Connecticut

In June 1686 King James II gave Andros a commission as governor of the new Dominion of New England. Despite an official protest from Connecticut, a third writ to Governor Treat delivered on December 28, 1686, informed him that Connecticut's charter must be surrendered. A month later Treat replied so politely that London interpreted it as full submission. In June 1687 instructions were prepared for Andros' assumption of power. As for Connecticut's assembly, it stalled on voting a clear-cut acceptance of Andros' rule.

Finally in October Andros decided to force a showdown. He wrote Treat that he planned to visit Hartford and take over the

69

government. Leaving Boston on October 26 in royal style with a retinue of seventy-five, he apparently expected no trouble with Connecticut. Governor Treat, affecting a friendly spirit, organized a splendid welcome for Andros. Interestingly, our most complete account of Andros' visit is found in Gershom Bulkeley's *Will and Doom*—a very pro-Andros version.

The next day Andros and his retinue accompanied the Governor and assembly to the meetinghouse where Andros had his commission and the order for surrender of the charter read. Governor Treat then began a very long and emotional speech describing the many trials and dangers involved in Connecticut's development. It grew dark and candles were lighted. Then occurred one of the most famous incidents in Connecticut's history.

> The important affair was debated and kept in suspense until the evening, when the charter was brought and laid upon the table, where the assembly were sitting. By this time, great numbers of people were assembled, and men sufficiently bold to enterprise whatever might be necessary or expedient. The lights were instantly extinguished, and one captain Wadsworth, of Hartford, in the most silent and secret manner, carried off the charter, and secreted it in a large hollow tree, fronting the house of the Hon. Samuel Wyllys, then one of the magistrates of the colony. The people appeared all peaceable and orderly. The candles were officiously relighted, but the patent was gone, and no discovery could be made of it, or of the person, who had conveyed it away.

This, the earliest printed account of this famous episode, appeared in 1797 in Benjamin Trumbull's first edition of his history. The secreting of the charter in the Charter Oak tree became one of Connecticut's most cherished traditions. Whether the charter ever was actually placed there remains an unsolved mystery. All that appears certain is that it *was* carried away somewhere under cover of darkness.

Despite its peculiar disappearance, both Andros and Connecticut leaders believed that Connecticut had been absorbed into the Dominion of New England. Andros added Governor Treat and Secretary John Allyn to his council, named justices of the peace and sheriffs and confirmed all recently levied taxes.

70

The Fall of the Dominion of New England

Despite Andros' protestations of deep friendship, he almost immediately imposed an autocratic government. Freedom of the press was restricted and enormous fees were levied for legal actions, including one of fifty shillings for probate of a will. Andros outraged many by his proclamation that all land titles under the 1662 charter were invalid, as well as all Indian deeds. In 1688 New York was added to his realm. In Massachusetts and Plymouth the weight of his oppressions fell even more heavily.

In England, meanwhile, a major crisis had developed between the arbitrary and unpopular King James II and Parliament. An avowed Catholic, James tried to dictate policy to the Church of England. When a son was born to James, it signified a Catholic heir. Leaders of both parties, Tories and Whigs, joined in an appeal to William, ruler of Holland, and his wife, Mary, daughter of James II by his first wife, both Protestants, to mount the English throne. James soon fled to France and the Glorious Revolution of 1688-89 moved ahead. William and Mary became rulers—but clearly subordinate to Parliament. Parliament had made a king, and easily could unmake him if he ruled arbitrarily. A bill of rights and other popular safeguards were enacted in confirming the revolutionary settlement.

The exciting news of revolution in England quickly precipitated revolution in New England. Actually, some Connecticut leaders, led by James Fitch of Norwich, apparently had been plotting against Andros for some time. In Boston on April 18, 1689, an armed mob seized Randolph and other Dominion supporters, but Andros escaped to Castle Island. Three weeks later, on May 9, 1689, the Connecticut legislature voted to re-establish their government under the charter of 1662. Governor Treat again assumed his place; and the assistants and deputies, theirs. Connecticut's own "Glorious Revolution" was completed!

References Consulted

Albert C. Bates, "Expedition of Sir Edmund Andros to Connecticut in 1687," *American Antiquarian Society Proceedings*, XLVIII (Oct. 1939)

Viola F. Barnes, *The Dominion of New England* (New Haven, 1923)

George W. Ellis and John E. Morris, *King Philip's War* . . . (New York, 1906)

Douglas E. Leach, *Flintlock and Tomahawk* (New York, 1958)

Herbert L. Osgood, *The American Colonies in the Seventeenth Century* (New York, 1930)

Benjamin Trumbull, *A Complete History of Connecticut* . . . (Hartford, 1797)

J. Hammond Trumbull, ed., *The Public Records of the Colony of Connecticut* . . . II, III (Hartford, 1852, 1859)

Alden T. Vaughan, *New England Frontier, Puritans and Indians, 1620-1675* (Boston, 1965)

VI Connecticut Fights in Four Intercolonial Wars -- 1690-1763

The Opening Round—King William's War

Britain's European diplomacy and wars inevitably deeply implicated the American colonies. The American phase of these wars involved the French and British colonies in a series of four wars, fought at intervals over a period of more than seventy years.

Connecticut men serving in these intercolonial wars came from the militia or trainbands. The militia, theoretically, included all men from sixteen to fifty. In 1762 there were about 20,000 militiamen in a white population of 141,000. Those exempted from service included assembly members, justices of the peace, ministers, Yale staff and students, masters of arts, doctors, schoolmasters, attorneys, millers, "constant Herdsmen," regular mariners and ferrymen, sheriffs, constables and lame or otherwise disabled persons.

Each of the thirteen regiments in 1750 had a colonel, lieutenant colonel and major—commissioned by the governor after appointment by the legislature. Lower officers were nominated by the men and normally confirmed automatically. The militiamen provided their own arms and drilled without pay, though fined for nonattendance.

The militia possessed a good reputation partly because, as a special committee reported to the assembly in 1754, their officers "generally are chosen out of the best yeomen of this colony." Connecticut's rejection of the Albany Plan of Union that year stemmed partly from fear of control over the militia by the president-general and council.

Since training was infrequent and often superficial, the militia comprised a force of uncertain quality. On occasion they fought well against the French; at worst they behaved like a rabble. Given Connecticut's traditions and outlook the militia provided a practical answer to current military needs.

The first war, called King William's War by Americans, grew out of serious French-English rivalry in such areas as Acadia, Newfoundland, Maine and the Illinois country. Under the aggressive leadership of Count Frontenac, the French organized attacks on

73

isolated frontier posts. The most serious foray, that on Schenectady in February 1689/90, left sixty dead and many captured.

Alarmed by these sharp attacks, Connecticut called out militia for an intercolonial land invasion of Canada. Of the five colonies which promised troops, only Connecticut provided its quota. From the start the expedition seemed jinxed. Smallpox and rotten pork disabled a substantial number of Connecticut troops. Finally, in view of a clearly hopeless situation, Fitz-John Winthrop, the expedition's commander, ordered a general retreat of the dispirited troops back to Albany. So the first Canadian invasion ended—a complete failure.

More dramatic than the struggle with the French and Indians was that with New York whose Governor Benjamin Fletcher, under authorization from the Lords of Trade, made Connecticut a satellite and claimed command of Connecticut's militia. In response, a special legislative session chose Fitz-John Winthrop as agent, and levied a special tax to finance his mission to England in defense of Connecticut's charter rights and the colony's control over its militia. Winthrop's mission to England lasted four years and although he was forced to accept some restrictions on Connecticut's privileges, he attained his central goal of retaining the colony's semiautonomous status within the empire.

In October 1693, meanwhile, Fletcher with some aides came to Hartford and demanded a "Yes or No" reply on his taking over the militia. The legislature replied "No," but offered money or men for New York's defense. Enraged, Fletcher again called for submission. According to tradition, he ordered his commission read to the Hartford militia parading nearby. Captain Joseph Wadsworth immediately cried out, "Beat the drums." After the great din ceased, Fletcher's aide again attempted to perform his duty, only to be drowned out by a second roll of drums. Noting the very defiant mood in Hartford, Fletcher thought it expedient to hasten his departure. As a parting criticism he asserted "I never sawe the like people."

In April 1694 London issued a decision partially supporting Connecticut's position. While upholding the charter provision giving command of the militia to the governor, it asserted that in time of crisis a chief commander over the militia of several colonies was legal. Fletcher was authorized to call out 120 Connecticut militia in war periods only, but Connecticut retained their control.

In 1697 with the Treaty of Ryswick the war officially ended in a virtual stalemate. News of peace was greeted with much jubilation and a day of public thanksgiving was celebrated. Fortunately, Connecticut lost few men though the war cost the treasury about £12,000.

The Second Round—Queen Anne's War

By 1702 an unresolved dispute over the succession to the Spanish throne once again plunged England into war with France—a conflict known in America as Queen Anne's War. Again Connecticut feared invasion by the French and their Indian allies. The concern was heightened by the action of the Iroquois, formerly English allies, who in 1701 made a peace agreement with Canada.

The war seemed remote to Connecticut, however, until the savage surprise attack made by French and Indians on Deerfield February 29, 1703/04. When the carnage ended, about fifty had perished and more than one hundred half-frozen captives were marched through the snow to Canada. This shocking raid sparked an emergency session of the General Assembly on March 15. It passed a series of preparedness measures, including the sending of sixty men for service in Hampshire County, Massachusetts. Later the assembly warned inhabitants of eight Connecticut frontier towns not to leave without obtaining prior legislative permission.

In 1707 Connecticut made a negative decision which proved fortunate. When asked by Governor Joseph Dudley of Massachusetts to contribute a large number of men for an expedition against Port Royal, Acadia, the assembly politely declined with a gentle reminder about earlier large assistance to Hampshire County. As a result, Connecticut escaped implication in the disgraceful debacle which followed. A second attempt also failed. In 1710 Britain and the colonials launched a new attack. In this venture Connecticut provided 300 troops under Colonel William Whiting and five transports. Under an effective commander, Colonel Francis Nicholson, the combined British-colonial forces on October 2, 1710, compelled French surrender of Port Royal without a battle.

The next venture, against Quebec, came to an unbelievable

denouement. A joint land-sea expedition was planned and Connecticut pledged its quota of 300 men. At a spot where the Gulf of St. Lawrence was about seventy miles wide ten ships succeeded in running aground, with huge losses of men! Though a force adequate to capture Quebec survived this miracle of incompetence, the expedition was abandoned. This action, in turn, terminated the land expedition. The Treaty of Utrecht in 1713 gave Britain Acadia, among other places.

Wartime expenditures resulted in Connecticut's first printing of paper money—an issue of £8,000 of bills of credit in June 1709. Later emissions raised the amount to £34,000 by May 1713. Succeeding wars pushed paper bills to much higher levels.

Round Three—King George's War

European peace held until the late 1730's when sharp Anglo-Spanish rivalry and strong jingoism led to the War of Jenkins' Ear against Spain in 1739. Britain hoped to injure the Spanish-American Empire by capturing Cartagena and other ports. For this expedition Connecticut provided enough volunteers to fill three transports. Woeful incompetence, disease and fierce Spanish opposition combined to doom the attack, and only a tiny percentage of the English colonials ever returned home.

In 1744 France and England became belligerents in a broader struggle called King George's War by Americans. Its most important engagement involved an expedition against the heavily-defended French fortress at Louisbourg on Cape Breton Island. This French base seemed to threaten New England's fishing and trading, and even the area's independence. When the prime promoter of an attack, Governor William Shirley of Massachusetts, asked Connecticut for assistance, he obtained a pledge of 500 fully-equipped men to serve under Deputy Governor Roger Wolcott.

The little Connecticut army, carried in seven transports, reached Nova Scotia successfully, despite a near-interception by a French frigate. After a close siege lasting seven weeks, the French surrendered on June 17, 1745. Wolcott exulted over the victory, calling it "such a conquest as we seldom meet with in history." For a change, the British officers praised the colonial performance!

To the extreme chagrin of the New Englanders, the Treaty of

76

Aix-la-Chapelle in 1748 returned all conquered territories to their former holders. New England felt that its dramatic services in helping to take Louisbourg had been callously ignored by British diplomats. In Connecticut a heavy loss of men and a war-incurred debt of £166,000 in new paper money heightened the resentment over Louisbourg's return. Despite the currency problem general economic activity was stimulated by supply contracts for the troops.

The Climax—the French and Indian War

The next decade saw British-French rivalry in America attain the highest level yet. Intense competition over trade, especially in the Ohio River Valley, erupted into open conflict in 1754, marked by George Washington's surrender at Fort Necessity.

That same year the Board of Trade, alarmed by a deterioration in relations with the Iroquois and other Indian allies, called a general congress at Albany to take urgent steps toward reinvigorating the alliances. Connecticut sent three delegates, William Pitkin, Elisha Williams and Roger Wolcott, with careful instructions warning against large commitments. After dealing with Indian problems, the congress adopted a proposal for a federal plan of intercolonial organization devised by Benjamin Franklin—the Albany Plan of Union.

Since Connecticut's delegates had officially objected to some aspects of the plan, it is hardly surprising that the assembly firmly rejected it on a number of grounds. The assembly resolution called the limits of the proposed union too great for the president-general and council to administer and defend successfully. The plan would hurt the King's interests, "subvert the liberties and privileges" of the people and reduce their industry. In the end, the plan was rejected by the colonies and London. Neither felt ready for a federal system which, in retrospect, might have postponed the American Revolution or made separation by peaceful evolutionary methods possible.

In 1755 British officials, frightened by the patent disloyalty of the French in Nova Scotia, suddenly deported 6,000 of them to many English colonies, including Connecticut. On January 21, 1756, the same day that the ship *Elizabeth* arrived at New London with 277 exiles, the assembly passed a humane act providing for care of

77

the Acadians. Fifty towns would share in housing arrangements and those too sick and infirm to travel would receive colony support. Some 700 Acadians actually entered Connecticut, where they seem to have received moderately good treatment. Always dreaming of returning to their homeland, in 1767 they began to leave Connecticut in substantial numbers. As an interesting sidelight, Nathaniel Shaw, Sr., of New London, a wealthy merchant, hired thirty-five destitute Acadians to build a handsome stone house—so solidly constructed that, as a historical museum, it welcomes visitors today.

The French and Indian War soon assumed large proportions. For an expedition against Crown Point in 1755, the colony contributed two regiments under Phineas Lyman. Part of this force under Colonel William Whiting suffered heavy losses in an ambush near Lake George. Shortly afterwards in the second of three clashes known collectively as the Battle of Lake George, the French struck hard at the colonial forces. When Sir William Johnson of New York, the commander, was wounded, Lyman assumed command and with great courage and skill checked the French until reinforcements arrived to rout them.

The next year Connecticut authorized no less than 3,300 men for the joint efforts against the French, but only the enemy achieved something—the capture of Oswego. The year 1757 brought further setbacks, although Connecticut furnished 1,400 men for the common effort. When news came that Fort William Henry faced imminent capture by Montcalm's besieging army, Connecticut rushed 5,000 more militia to the fort's rescue. En route there Connecticut's soldiers met half-naked fugitives fleeing from a brutal Indian massacre after the fort fell. Since Montcalm's army had burned the fort, Connecticut militia returned home.

The series of calamitous defeats inflicted on Britain caused a change in government and assumption of power in 1757 by William Pitt as Prime Minister. Infusing a new vigor into the war effort, Pitt asked for larger colonial forces. Connecticut responded by calling up four regiments, 5,000 men in all, under Lyman. Given Pitt's inspiring leadership, the tide of war dramatically turned in 1758. General Jeffrey Amherst, supplied with an impressive army of regulars and colonials and supported by a fleet, conducted an efficient siege of Louisbourg, which resulted in surrender on July 26, 1758.

Fort Duquesne and Fort Frontenac also capitulated to British troops.

On another front, the invasion of Canada via the Champlain Valley, affairs went badly from the start. Although Connecticut troops under Lyman performed valiantly, General James Abercromby provided such dismal leadership that nothing was accomplished. In contempt the colonials nicknamed their commander "Mrs. Nabbycromby!"

Undismayed by Abercromby's fiasco, Pitt laid plans for a decisive American campaign in 1759. When asked for 5,000 troops, Connecticut voted 3,600 men; and later, under pressure, 1,000 more. Serving under General Amherst, Lyman's men participated in the reduction of Ft. Ticonderoga. Less than two months later General James Wolfe earned his greatest victory in the stirring battle on the Plains of Abraham, after which Quebec fell on September 17, 1759. The French and Indian War reached its closing chapter in 1760 with the expedition against Montreal, in which Connecticut forces took part. When Amherst's army was stopped at Oswegatchie by two French vessels, Colonel Israel Putnam of Connecticut led a force of 1,000 men, stripped to the waist, who quickly swarmed over the two ships. Early in September Amherst's army, joined by other British forces, overcame the French. In the Treaty of Paris of 1763 Britain took all French possessions in America except a few islands.

For Connecticut the war since 1757 had involved military service for about twenty percent of the able-bodied men. From 1755 through March 1764 the colony printed £346,500 in bills of credit, but taxed heavily enough to pay off all except £82,000 by early 1764. Parliamentary reimbursement and major army contracts helped to keep the colony prosperous—so much so that no taxes were levied from 1766 through 1769. In terms of military contributions Connecticut ranked at or near the top among the English colonies.

References Consulted

James Truslow Adams, *Revolutionary New England* (Boston, 1923)

Samuel A. Drake, *The Border Wars of New England* . . . (New York, 1897)

Lawrence H. Gipson, *The British Empire Before the American Revolution*, V, *Zones of International Friction* . . . *1748-1754;* VI, *The Great War for the Empire: The Years of Defeat, 1754-1757* (New York, 1942, 1946)

Charles J. Hoadly, ed., *The Public Records of the Colony of Connecticut* . . . IV, V, VIII, IX, X, XI (Hartford, 1868, 1870, 1874, 1876, 1879, 1880)

John S. McLennan, *Louisbourg, from its Foundation to its Fall, 1713-1758* (London, 1918)

Curtis Nettels, *The Roots of American Civilization* (New York, 1938)

Edmund O'Callaghan, ed., *Documents Relative to the Colonial History of the State of New-York* . . . IV (Albany, 1854)

Herbert L. Osgood, *The American Colonies in the Eighteenth Century* (New York, 1930)

Benjamin Trumbull, *A Complete History of Connecticut* . . . (New London, 1898)

VII Earning a Living

Farming—Connecticut's Chief Occupation

From the earliest days of the colony most men found it necessary to cultivate the soil. The fertile soil of the Connecticut River Valley had provided the major lure for the three earliest English settlements. As time passed, occupations became more diversified, but to the end of the colonial period most artisans and professional men farmed part time.

It is interesting to note that the early settlements were made in the warmer parts of Connecticut—the coast and the Connecticut River Valley. Even here the growing season—about six months—is relatively short.

Extremes of precipitation—droughts and floods—always have been rare. Precipitation, then presumably as now, was distributed fairly evenly throughout the year and totaled about forty-five inches annually. Other than rockiness and thinness of soil in upland areas there were no major obstacles to establishment of an agrarian society. Those who settled in the more fertile river valleys and coastal lowlands, however, found farming easier and more profitable.

In pioneer times settlers discovered that maize, or Indian corn, constituted a highly dependable food so it became the chief crop. Usually farmers planted it in hills three or four feet apart and often used fish as fertilizer. An ancient rhyme depicts the fate of corn kernels:

> One for the bug,
> One for the crow,
> One to rot,
> And two to grow.

By late colonial times farmers with good soil realized yields of twenty to twenty-five bushels per acre. Since corn was relatively simple to plant and cultivate, it was grown in all parts of the colony.

In 1680 the governor and council received a questionnaire from London. Their reply included a succinct picture of agriculture. Indian corn, peas, rye, wheat, wool, flax, hemp, barley, pork, beef,

81

apple cider and pear cider (parry) were listed as the principal agricultural products. In an answer of 1762 to new queries from London the governor and council enumerated a similar list of exports, but added flour, bread, horses, some cattle, sheep, swine and oats. They considered pork and beef as their staples.

By the late colonial period most farmers still raised large amounts of corn, beans, peas, squash, pumpkins and turnips, while Wethersfield specialized in onions. Apples were very popular, especially when changed into cider and "apple-jack," or brandy!

One of Connecticut's earliest crops was tobacco, probably grown in Windsor by 1640. The settlers then grew the same leaf —*poke* or *ottomauch*—raised by valley Indians. Because of its bitter taste colonists later replaced it with a milder West Indian variety. By 1700 an export trade in tobacco leaf had developed, but after 1750 tobacco income slumped because of Virginia competition and wars.

About 1750 a basic change occurred in Connecticut's agriculture—a shift from soil tillage to grazing. Expanding markets in the West Indies and mainland colonies encouraged farmers to expand production of cattle, horses, mules, sheep and hogs. Increasingly farmers planted red clover, timothy and other English grasses which insured fatter livestock. Cattle from Vermont and New York were driven to Connecticut for fattening up through the winter, spring and summer for fall sale. Also, the by-products, butter and cheese, were exported to the South and the West Indies.

In the beginning of the economic revolution in Connecticut during the second half of the century, considerable geographical specialization developed. Rye, flaxseed, wheat and onions were cultivated in river valleys and lowlands. Rye and oats were raised in the valley, inland New Haven and Fairfield counties and the limestone area of Litchfield County. While grain was mostly consumed in the colony, some was exported and by the late 1760's the export of flour had become substantial. In Fairfield and New Haven counties and the Connecticut Valley, farmers produced much flaxseed and sent some to New York City where part of it was exported to Ireland. Flaxseed was so valuable that one barrel often was traded for two of salt.

The boom in meat and dairy products reflected growing de-

82

The David Judson House (1723) at Stratford—a comfortable home of a well-to-do family.

mand plus the fact that livestock could be pastured almost anywhere in the colony, including the hilly rocky areas of the eastern and western highlands.

In 1760 Nathaniel Aspinwall brought cuttings from mulberry trees to Mansfield and started an orchard. He and Ezra Stiles of New Haven provided the leadership in establishing a silk industry which was centered in Mansfield but spread to other towns.

Unfortunately agricultural practices in Connecticut, as in other colonies, generally were inefficient. Given scarce and expensive labor, abundant land, primitive tools and limited markets, farmers practiced *extensive* agriculture—the use of small amounts of labor and fertilizer applied to large amounts of land. Frequently the seed was poor, also. Gradually tools were improving as rakes, scythes, forks, flails and harrows began to appear. The sturdy patient oxen continued as the farmer's most reliable servant, though horses were becoming fairly common.

Like a voice crying in the wilderness came the recommendations of Jared Eliot, Killingworth clergyman, who wrote and spoke for improved agricultural methods to restore worn-out lands, drain bogs and develop a staple such as hemp.

To the end of the colonial period many families practiced subsistence farming; kept some livestock; raised food, wool and flax; made their own clothing as well as tools and simple furniture; and because of dire lack of cash tried desperately to be self-sufficient. By the mid-century many farmers were beginning to produce enough surplus, especially livestock, beef, pork, dairy products, flaxseed and onions, to provide goods for export trade. Thus they earned income to purchase much-coveted English manufactures, mostly through Boston and New York.

The Beginnings of Manufacturing

While every farm family practiced manufacturing at home in producing implements for home use, manufacturing in the sense of turning out articles in quantity for sale in a local or distant market remained limited.

In a typical agricultural village the gristmill was usually the first authorized manufacturing enterprise. The early undershot mills, located on small streams, performed small-scale grinding of grain. Later, as population grew, higher-capacity mills, often of the overshot type, were constructed on larger streams. Similarly sawmills became common, as a grant in 1653 to John Winthrop, Jr., in New London indicated.

Aware of the great profits in England's growing trade, the legislature passed acts to encourage flax growing for cloth, and hemp for cordage and canvas. A few fulling mills for finishing cloth appeared in such places as East Hartford and Stamford. In 1766 at Norwich enterprising Christopher Leffingwell initiated two businesses—papermaking and stocking-weaving. Soon afterwards he built fulling mills and a chocolate factory.

As early as 1638 Thomas Nash of New Haven launched Connecticut's clock industry. Little more progress was made, however, until 1726 when Ebenezer Parmele built a tower clock for Guilford's meetinghouse. Colonial clockmakers of distinction included Benjamin Cheney, Seth Young(s) and Thomas Harland. Over forty clockmakers made clocks, some of which still grace Connecticut homes and museums.

One other industry, ironmaking, became solidly established in the colonial era. In the 1650's promoters instituted ironmaking at East Haven and New London—efforts which greatly interested John Winthrop, Jr. It was not until many decades later, however, that Connecticut's best iron deposits were discovered in the northwest. In 1732 an iron mine was opened at Ore Hill, Salisbury, and in 1734, a forge at nearby Lime Rock. Prior to the Revolution new blast furnaces began operations at Canaan, Kent, Lakeville and Roxbury.

Shipbuilding Flourishes in Connecticut

Bringing in more income than most industries was shipbuilding. Blessed with abundant timber and numerous navigable rivers and protected coastal ports, Connecticut early began building small vessels for the coastal and West Indian trades. Usually a small family enterprise, shipbuilding provided supplementary revenue. Often a vessel was started in the fall after the harvest and completed early in the spring. The most popular types constructed were ketches and sloops—small craft with one mast and fore-and-aft sails. In the later colonial years larger two-masted vessels of the brig, brigantine and snow types became popular. Some demand existed, also, for the bark and schooner—a type increasingly popular in the eighteenth century.

In the 1660's John Coit established New London's first shipbuilding business with construction of three small barks. Through the years the Coits constructed many small vessels. Joshua Hempsted's *Diary* notes that he worked in the Coit shipyard. In January 1712/13 Hempsted himself agreed to build a complete thirty-five foot sloop for £65—payable half in money and half in goods. The Coits and others kept New London in the forefront of shipbuilding. Numerous other towns such as Norwich, New Haven, Branford, Guilford, Fairfield, Stratford, Saybrook, Essex, Middle Haddam, Middletown, Rocky Hill, Glastonbury, Wethersfield and Hartford kept shipbuilders busy, also.

Courtesy of Mystic Seaport. Photo by Louis S. Martel

Colonial topsail schooner.

The 1756 account of Connecticut vessels, prepared for the Board of Trade, affords a good breakdown. It lists by name seventy-four vessels with a tonnage of 3,202 and crews totaling 415. The vessels ranged from 15 tons burden to 90, with those around 40 tons the most common. Crews numbered from 3 to 10, with 6 the most prevalent size.

Because of abundant timber, New Englanders could construct vessels for about thirty percent less than the English. Occasionally Connecticut vessels were sold abroad after their owners had profited from the outward cargo. Normally, however, owners used their vessel for ten to fifteen years before rot overcame the timbers, if indeed shipwreck or other catastrophes had not intervened.

Connecticut's Enterprising Merchants

From the early colonial days Connecticut Yankees engaged in trading. A typical farmer brought his surplus corn, pork, beef, rye, oats, tallow, staves, livestock, vegetables, apples and cider to the local storekeeper. These products were bartered with him for stock usually described as "European" and "West Indian," meaning goods such as sugar, molasses, rum, spices, indigo, many kinds of cloth, glassware, powder, shot, guns, wines and bar iron. The shopkeeper in turn took his produce, or "country pay," plus occasional small amounts of cash to the merchant of a larger town, such as Middletown or New Haven, where he exchanged it for needed European and West Indian goods. The town merchant then sent most of the goods received from country shopkeepers and his own local customers to a major importing center such as Boston, New York or possibly Newport. There he purchased English goods from one of the importing or "sedentary" merchants. Because of the chronic severe shortage of coins, a larger percentage of trade was conducted on a credit basis while direct barter gradually declined.

Famous Connecticut storekeepers included Benedict Arnold and Roger Sherman. Attracted by the remarkably rapid growth of population and trade in New Haven, Sherman left New Milford to settle there. In 1760 he opened a store which he managed skillfully for over a decade. He carried a varied stock including dry goods, ribbons, silks, spices, books and pamphlets and seems to have prospered. One of the greatest problems facing Sherman and other merchants was the unstable and depreciating paper money from Rhode Island and New Hampshire which debtors eagerly forced upon them. In 1752 Sherman vigorously expressed his views in a pamphlet denouncing those currencies and demanding assembly legislation to prohibit their use. That very year the assembly declared recent Rhode Island bills of credit illegal, and in 1755 outlawed specific issues of both Rhode Island and New Hampshire bills of credit.

Although peddlers are commonly associated with Connecticut, actually they seem to have been frequently unpopular. In 1757 the legislature voted to require them to secure a license for which a five pound fee was required and provide penalties for unlicensed peddling. To provide tighter control in 1765 the assembly raised the license fee to twenty pounds.

While Connecticut lacked a powerful mercantile aristocracy of the type which Boston and Philadelphia boasted, scattered among about twenty towns one could find a significant group of substantial merchants. If Connecticut had a "merchant prince" prior to the Revolution, it was probably Nathaniel Shaw, Jr., of New London. Over the years he built up a complex network of commercial correspondents along the coast, in the West Indies and even in London. He traded extensively with such men and firms as Peter Vandervoort (New York City), Thomas and Isaac Wharton (Philadelphia), Joshua Elderkin (Windham), Josiah Waters (Boston), Christopher Champlin (Newport), William Packwood (Martinique), John and Michael Dykers (St. Eustatius), John Hodson (Amsterdam) and Lane and Booth (London).

In the voluminous Shaw papers at Yale one can examine innumerable voyages and transactions in which Shaw engaged. In 1769, for instance, a Shaw vessel, the *Lucretia*, sailed for the West Indies with a cargo consisting of 48 horses, 15,000 pine boards, 148 shaken casks, 8,000 hoops, 2,300 staves, 28 barrels of beef, 8 barrels of pork, 9 tierces of bread, 11 tons of hay, 600 bushels of oats, 68 casks of water and sundries—the entire cargo valued at £894.14.0.

This particular cargo typified those carried from Connecticut to the West Indies. In return Connecticut vessels brought molasses, sugar, salt, tropical fruits and much-sought bills of exchange. All reports agree that while the coastal trade was extensive, the West

Indian trade produced the largest profits. Connecticut merchants usually traded directly with the West Indies instead of making them part of a triangle involving Europe or Africa. Favorite destinations were British Barbados, Antigua, Grenada, St. Kitts and Jamaica; French Guadeloupe and Martinique; Dutch St. Eustatius; and Spanish Hispaniola. For salt shippers frequented Turks Island, among other places.

The West Indian trade mainly prospered after 1700 because of the increasing popularity of rum among the masses. While the wealthier preferred West India rum, the Connecticut distilleries made increasing quantities of New England rum for ordinary people.

Since sugar remained expensive, molasses found increasing favor as a cheaper sweetener. This stepped-up demand for molasses in turn encouraged Connecticut merchants to seek it at lower prices in the foreign West Indies, especially Guadeloupe and Martinique. The Molasses Act of 1733 placed a high duty on foreign molasses, but because of lax enforcement had little impact on Connecticut.

Many recommended a direct trade with Britain but few Connecticut merchants dared to try. Among the few was Jonathan Trumbull of Lebanon, the future governor, who in 1750, joined Elisha Williams and Joseph Pitkin as Williams, Trumbull and Pitkin. The firm never prospered and was terminated after Williams' death in 1755. In early 1764 Trumbull joined with his son Joseph and Eleazer Fitch of Windham in a new partnership, Trumbull, Fitch and Trumbull. Among other activities this firm traded with two major London firms—Lane and Booth, and Champion and Hayley. They also imported varied English goods through Boston. Unfortunately a lethal combination of bad markets, nonpaying debtors, sunken ships and plain mismanagement wrecked the firm's financial position and plunged Trumbull into unofficial bankruptcy by the late 1760's. His election as governor in 1769 came just in time to prevent an overwhelming onslaught by creditors. Nathaniel Shaw, Jr., on the other hand, apparently made some money out of his English ventures.

Many merchants invested in the coastal trade which earlier had been dominated by Boston. By the late colonial period New York had wrested first place from Boston. From 1758-67 even New

London reported far more trade with New York than Boston. Unable to purchase European goods directly, Connecticut merchants relied on New York and Boston importers.

A traveler to Connecticut around 1760 vividly likened the colony "to a cask of good liquor, tapped at both ends, at one of which Boston draws, and New York at the other, till little is left in it but lees and settlings." Although Joseph Trumbull prepared a comprehensive plan aimed at ending Connecticut's dependence on New York and Boston, he conceded that "most of our Traders know nothing of Trade in any other way, and have been so long in it, they are like a Horse in mill, they keep on the same beaten way, without Turning to the Right Hand or the left."

Some Connecticut merchants, however, traded with other places besides New York and Boston. To the east they found growing profits at Halifax and other Nova Scotian ports, Falmouth (Portland), Piscataqua (Portsmouth), Salem, Nantucket, Newport and Providence. To the south Connecticut captains frequently visited Philadelphia, Annapolis, Chesapeake Bay and the Carolinas.

Typically, in order to spread risks, several persons owned a vessel and shared profits or losses. Even the cargoes were varied to avoid having a large amount of one article produce a glutted market. The captain of a small Connecticut sloop was allowed wide latitude as to where and for how much he sold his cargo, and what he secured for the return cargo. The captain and sometimes other crew members were often permitted a "privilege" of shipping a few goods as a private speculation.

Connecticut still exhibited a very provincial outlook, but its rapidly expanding trade was widening the intellectual horizons of the people. While only a small percentage of its citizens actively participated in maritime activities, they changed Connecticut from a scattered area of agricultural villages to a colony involved in the world. The mariners, moreover, sold much surplus produce and thus elevated many farmers from meager subsistence farming to comfortable standards of living. The import of English manufactures vastly increased daily living comfort. Maritime-related economic activities such as shipbuilding and repairing, sail and ropemaking and retailing all added substantially to the income of port towns.

90

Other Occupations Unimportant

A comparative handful of men earned a living in other ways. There always was fishing in the lakes, rivers, the Sound and the open ocean, but it was generally only a supplementary source of income. Connecticut never approached the level of Massachusetts which had superb fishing grounds much closer. Since there was no regular army or navy, no military class existed, except as militia served in wartime. A small but important professional class was developing slowly. With increasing trade and business generally the legal profession was growing. With the strong Puritan commitment to education, teachers were fairly numerous. Physicians still were very scarce, but held an honored place in society. Overall farming clearly dominated as the means of livelihood.

References Consulted

Robert G. Albion, William A. Baker, and Benjamin W. Labaree, *New England and the Sea* (Middletown, 1972)

Percy W. Bidwell and John I. Falconer, *History of Agriculture in the Northern United States, 1620-1860* (Washington, 1925)

James L. Bishop, *A History of American Manufactures from 1608 to 1860* . . . (Philadelphia, 1866)

Frances M. Caulkins, *History of Norwich, Connecticut* . . . (Hartford, 1866)

Christopher Collier, *Roger Sherman's Connecticut, Yankee Politics and the American Revolution* (Middletown, 1971)

Timothy Dwight, *Travels in New-England and New-York,* I-III (New Haven, 1821-22)

Jared Eliot, *Essays upon Field Husbandry in New England* . . . (New York, 1934)

Roland M. Hooker, *The Colonial Trade of Connecticut,* Connecticut Tercentenary Commission Publications, No. 50 (New Haven, 1936)

Margaret E. Martin, *Merchants and Trade of the Connecticut River Valley, 1750-1820* (Northampton, 1939)

Albert L. Olson, *Agricultural Economy and the Population in Eighteenth-Century Connecticut,* Connecticut Tercentenary Commission Publications, No. 40 (New Haven, 1935)

Gaspare J. Saladino, "The Economic Revolution in Late Eighteenth Century Connecticut" (Unpublished Ph.D. dissertation, Wisconsin, 1964)

Glenn Weaver, *Jonathan Trumbull, Connecticut's Merchant Magistrate (1710-1785)* (Hartford, 1956)

———— "Some Aspects of Early Eighteenth-Century Connecticut's Trade," *Connecticut Historical Society Bulletin, XXII* (January 1957)

VIII Society of Colonial Connecticut

A Burgeoning Population

In common with other English colonies Connecticut enjoyed very rapid population growth. Estimated at 800 persons in 1636 and 2,000 in 1640, it had jumped to about 12,000 by 1675; perhaps 30,000 by 1701; and to 130,612 in the first census—that of January 1, 1756. No later census is available until 1774, but a reply to the Board of Trade in 1774 indicated a population of about 145,500 in 1762. The list of ten most populous towns for 1756 offers contrasts to the present.

TEN MOST POPULOUS TOWNS WITH TAX LISTS

Town	1756 Census	1756 Tax Assessment	Rank in Assessment
1 Middletown	5,664	£48,692	4
2 Norwich	5,540	58,008	1
3 New Haven	5,085	54,141	2
4 Fairfield	4,455	50,762	3
5 Windsor	4,220	40,400	8
6 Wallingford	3,713	41,205	7
7 Farmington	3,707	43,094	6
8 Stratford	3,658	43,100	5
9 Stonington	3,518	35,660	10
10 Lebanon	3,274	39,749	9

The high value of the assessments in New Haven and Norwich suggests the relative prosperity of those two bustling ports—active in coastal and West Indian trade.

Connecticut's black population in 1756 totaled 3,019—or 2.3 percent of the total. They were most numerous in Fairfield (260), Norwich (223), Middletown (218) and Stonington (200). All evidence indicates that the great majority were slaves.

Only a small remnant of Connecticut's once proud Indian population had survived to 1756. The census revealed just 617 Indians in three towns—Stonington (365), Groton (158) and Lyme (94).

It is interesting to note that in 1756 Hartford had only 3,027 inhabitants and Waterbury, just 1,829. Obviously no town approached in size what the modern word "city" suggests. In fact, the modest population figures for each town included its entire area—much of which was rural in nature.

The population was concentrated along Long Island Sound with fingers up the Connecticut River, Thames River to Norwich and Housatonic and Naugatuck Rivers. In the Eastern and Western Highlands it thinned out rapidly. Poor rockier soils partly explain this; but for Litchfield County, which in places possessed rich lime-stone-based soils, one finds the explanation in late settlement. The entire county claimed only 11,827 and just one relatively populous town—Woodbury. This county was Connecticut's last frontier, but even it was filling rapidly by the 1750's.

Family Life

To understand a society well one must examine its family life. The Puritans held the happily-married and devoted couple in great honor. Thomas Hooker wrote with great sensitivity about conjugal love, as this sample indicates:

> That the Husband tenders his Spouse with an indeared affec-
> tion above al mortal creatures: This appeares by the expressions of
> his respect, that all he hath, is at her command, al he can do, is
> wholly improved for her content and comfort, she lies in his Bosom,
> and his heart trusts in her, which forceth al to confess, that the
> stream of his affection, like a mighty current, runs with ful Tide
> and strength.

To Puritans the family structure was strictly hierarchical. The husband rated superior to the wife; parents, to children; and masters, to servants or slaves. This was considered divinely ordained.

Puritans deemed it necessary to control marriage from the start. To prevent young couples from contracting rash and unwise marriages, in 1640 Connecticut became the only colony requiring espousals by law. Eight days in advance of entering into a contract of espousals occurred the required publication of the banns—public announcement of intent to marry. Once this contract was signed, eight more days must elapse before the actual marriage ceremony. Everywhere in New England an engaged couple was set apart and considered as all but married.

In its Code of 1650 Connecticut insisted that youth under age and still under control of parents or guardians must not enter into espousal and marriage without parental or guardian permission. Amusingly enough, the Code specifically forbade third parties to "intermeddle" in marriage plans!

Connecticut Puritans considered marriage a civil ceremony to be performed by a local magistrate—an injunction not lifted until 1686. Usually the final public event was a party where much feasting and drinking enlivened the scene. Under the Dominion of New England ministers first were authorized to perform marriages, though Connecticut did not enact legislation to this effect until 1694. Given this sanction many young ladies preferred the religious ceremony and more impressive setting for a wedding in the meetinghouse, filled with relatives and friends.

Then as today, occasionally a man and woman preferred living together without benefit of clergy. In New London, according to tradition, the Reverend Gurdon Saltonstall encountered such an infamous couple. Immediately he questioned them thus: "Do you really, John, take this your servant-maid, bought with your money, for your wife? Do you, Mary, take this man so much older than yourself for your husband?" Obtaining an affirmative reply from both, he replied: "Then I pronounce you, according to the laws of this colony, man and wife." Whereupon John shook his head and replied, "Ah, Gurdon! Thou art a cunning creature."

While there were few impediments to a lawful marriage, Connecticut made it difficult to obtain a divorce. Marriage was considered a permanent union not to be severed until death, except for extraordinary cause. In the early years a sprinkling of divorces was granted. An early case in 1655 concerned Goody Beckwith of Fairfield whose husband had deserted her. Mrs. Beckwith was ordered to submit her evidence to the magistrate's court at Stratford with authorization to said court to grant a divorce.

Cases of desertion continued to arise occasionally. In 1677 Mary Murrain, wife of Patrick Murrain, charged that he had willfully deserted her for over six years. The assembly then declared her divorced "w[i]th liberty to disspose herselfe in marriage, as God shall grant her oppertunety."

It was not always the woman who felt aggrieved. In 1657 Robert Wade of Saybrook petitioned for divorce on grounds that for fifteen years his wife Elizabeth had refused to live with him, either in England or Connecticut. The Court decided that Wade had exercised sufficient patience and granted the divorce!

After several decades of handling divorce cases on an individual basis, in 1677 the legislature enacted a general statute. This established adultery, fraudulent contract, willful desertion for three years with complete neglect of duty or seven years "providentiall absence" without communication (constituting legal death) as grounds for divorce.

Though extreme cruelty was not specifically listed as grounds, the assembly could find it adequate cause. In 1753 Mary Larkum charged her husband with conduct so "barbarous and inhuman" that she feared for her very life. On being summoned before the assembly Job Larkum admitted the charges. They thereupon promptly granted the divorce.

Both Connecticut and New Haven made adultery a capital offense. In practice, the death penalty was considered too extreme, but fines, whippings, brandings and wearing of a letter "A" were common punishments.

While legally parental authority over children's marriage was large, it still was limited. They might prevent a young man from courting their daughter, withhold a child's dowry and even deny permission for marriage; yet they were not supposed to force a child into an unwanted marriage. To be good Puritan parents they must respect the preferences of their children. In practice, both parents and children should consent to a match.

John Winthrop, Jr.'s, children seem to have amicably accepted the guidance of their parents. Yet a few decades later in 1707, Fitz-John Winthrop, a son of the governor, declared that it was the custom of the country for young folks to make their own choice of a mate, and except in case of major disqualification the community acceded. Obviously Puritan youth were moving away from passive acceptance of parental choice.

While parents less and less determined the choice, they often haggled disgracefully over the financial terms of the proposed marriage. Edmund S. Morgan finds evidence that a girl's parents normally gave only half as much dowry as the boy's.

Many writers have quoted Sarah Kemble Knight's statement that males in Connecticut more often married under twenty years than over. No careful statistical study of marriage yet has been published for colonial Connecticut, but studies of Plymouth and Andover, Massachusetts, indicate marriages took place later than usually thought. In Plymouth the mean age of first marriage for men born in the 1600-1700 period ranged downward from 27 to 24.6; for women in the same period, a rising trend from 20.6 to 22.3. In Andover the average age at marriage of men in the second and third generations was 26.7 and 27.1 respectively; for women, 22.3 and 24.5.

Late marriage resulted partly from the lengthy wait necessary to acquire enough land to support a family. Many fathers sought to retain control over their children by not distributing their land except by will. New England farms were small and often became smaller when a father divided his land among two or more sons. There could be relief, however, if a town decided to parcel out any remaining undivided land.

While colonial families of amazing size, 15 to 20 or more children, existed, they seem to have been rare. In Andover the average number of children in all families in the first two generations was approximately eight, of which seven reached age twenty-one. It seems likely that Connecticut families of this period would have had similar numbers of children.

In the nucleated agricultural towns which dotted the Connecticut landscape the patriarchal family lived with its ideals of hierarchy, order and tight community. Very possibly the strong controls instituted by parents seemed necessary in a household often numbering ten to a dozen or more, when one considers that sundry grandparents, uncles and aunts might also be living in the household.

At an early age the children learned that idle hands were sinful. Girls cared for infants, sewed, cooked, cleaned, spun flax, combed wool and generally helped their hard-pressed mothers. Boys chopped wood and brought it in, fed and watered the livestock, picked berries, weeded, gathered vegetables, spooled yarn and ran a variety of errands. Some sons were bound out as an apprentice to learn a trade. Undoubtedly a son often hunted or fished with his father.

Despite the intense emphasis on work children managed to

96

play games surprisingly like some of those still enjoyed. A book of the Revolutionary period lists such games and pastimes as kiteflying, hop-skip-and-jump, swimming, leapfrog, hopscotch and target-shooting. Children's toys, while rare, were sold and a few dolls and other items have survived.

Religious families had prayers and the daily reading of scriptures. According to the Code of 1650 parents were required at least weekly to catechize all children and servants on the principles of religion. From daily exposure to the Bible many children must have known it well.

To children of today, usually brought up permissively, the severely-disciplined Puritan child, circumscribed by so many "do's" and "don'ts," may seem unfortunate. Yet there is little evidence that Puritan children seriously suffered from parental strictness. They expected rigorous discipline and their familial responsibilities usually were clearly delineated, with failures promptly punished. In the large families then prevalent the authoritarian regime had the virtue, too, of preventing complete chaos in everyday living. Despite austere living conditions the Connecticut family found rich and enduring values in its living patterns.

Blacks in Connecticut

The institution of slavery apparently began soon after the River Colony and New Haven were established. Edward Hopkins and George Wyllys of Hartford, and John Davenport and Theophilus Eaton of New Haven owned slaves, as did other well-to-do settlers. Eaton seems to have justified his ownership of at least three slaves by reference to the Biblical term "strangers." Apparently he felt that it was justifiable to impose slavery on those not embracing true religion.

Negro slavery never attained large dimensions in any part of New England. No staple crop required gangs of workers, as did tobacco or rice. The indentured servant system seemed a far better method to meet the section's acute need for a larger labor force and was widely used. At an early date New England developed trade with the West Indian islands which already had a well-established slave system. Inevitably traders from that area sought to sell surplus slaves. Puritans had mixed feelings about the morality of slavery, but public opinion at least tolerated the institution. Captivity of Indians as a result of a just war was considered proper, and some Pequots were made slaves. Others were shipped to Providence Island. In return Negro slaves were brought from that island to Massachusetts. If Massachusetts could condone slavery, is it surprising that Connecticut emulated the colony which so often served as its model?

The earliest official information about slavery appears in 1680 in Connecticut's reply to queries from London—it reported not over thirty slaves. Usually only three or four yearly were imported from Barbados at a price averaging about £22 apiece.

By 1690 Connecticut had enough Negroes to precipitate legislation forbidding them to wander outside the town's boundaries without a special pass from their master or the town's authority. Ferrymen particularly were ordered to insist on the pass. The master was liable for costs incurred in returning his slave.

It is apparent that at an early date some slaveholders had manumitted their slaves, often after many years of service. Reluctant to have the towns pay for freedmen who needed financial relief, the legislature in 1702 declared the former owner liable for any costs involved. In its operation this law might well serve to discourage manumission.

The preamble to an assembly act of 1708 suggests a significant increase in the number of slaves by that time:

> And whereas negro and molatto servants or slaves are become numerous in some parts of this Colonie, and are very apt to be turbulent, and often quarrelling with white people to the great disturbance of the peace . . .

The act provided that if a slave or servant disturbed the peace or struck a white person, he would incur a penalty of whipping, to a maximum of thirty stripes for a single offense.

On April 15, 1708, the Lords of Trade wrote Connecticut requesting information on such matters as the number of Negroes annually imported directly from Africa, by whom and the rates charged. The governor and council replied that from June 1698 to December 1707 not a single vessel of any type had transported Negroes from Africa to Connecticut. They reported only a few Negroes, who usually were supplied from neighboring provinces except occasionally a half dozen or so yearly imported from the West Indies. While Connecticut's replies often were uninformative, probably this one accurately represented the situation.

A few years later in 1723 the assembly considered it necessary to prohibit Negroes and Indians from moving about after 9 P.M. at night except when under specific orders from their masters. A punishment of up to ten stripes and court costs awaited the violator. Anybody entertaining such wanderers in his home after 9 P.M. rendered himself liable to a fine of twenty shillings.

The famous journal of Mrs. Sarah Kemble Knight of Boston revealed not only Mrs. Knight's outlook on racial relations in 1704-05 but also the prevalence of an easy informality in Connecticut.

> And they Generally lived very well and comfortably in their famelies. But too Indulgent (especially the farmers) to their slaves: sufering too great familiarity from them, permitting them to sit at Table and eat with them, (as they say to save time,) and into the dish goes the black hoof as freely as the white hand. They told me that there was a farmer . . . who had some difference with his slave, concerning something the master had promised him and did not punctualy perform; w[hi]ch caused some hard words between them; But at length they put the matter to Arbitration and Bound themselves to stand to the award of such as they named—w[hi]ch done, the Arbitrators Having heard the Allegations of both parties, Order the master to pay 40s to black face, and acknowledge his fault. And so the matter ended: the poor master very honestly standing to the award.

In Connecticut's diversified agricultural economy of small farms even the more prosperous farmers could use only one to three slaves. Many actually worked *beside* a master and not just *for* him. If the master spent time in nonagricultural occupations such as fishing, shipbuilding, lumbering and trading, he might use his slave as an assistant there, also.

The largest slaveholder in colonial Connecticut apparently was Godfrey Malbone who after mercantile reverses in Newport, Rhode Island, retired to a large estate in the Brooklyn society of Pomfret. Educated at Queen's College, Oxford; much traveled; and a stanch Anglican, he attempted to live the life of an aristocrat even in rural Brooklyn. In 1764 his estate included twenty-seven Negroes. In his later life, returns on his slave labor became so poor that costs exceeded profits. Ellen Larned, Windham County historian, described his slaves in these terms:

They were a happy, jolly set, fond of fiddling and frolicking. Once a year they held a grand jubilee, electing a *king,* and installing him in office. Pero, the most intelligent of their number, son of an African king, usually obtained their suffrages and received royal homage. Some of these negroes left their master during the Revolution.

Other prominent Connecticut leaders also possessed **Negro** slaves. Larned refers to Eliphalet Dyer in Windham as having a "houseful of negroes, great and small." Norwich had an unusually large number of blacks—partly free and partly slave. In the early 1700's the price for slaves ranged from 60 shillings to £30. Captain **John Perkins** at the time of his death in 1761 had **fifteen slaves** which placed him among the largest slaveholders of the colony. In Norwich the Negroes for many years staged a mock election of a black governor. Their masters provided food, liquor and decorations for the ceremonial affair which provided much pleasure, excitement and sometimes disorder.

From John Davenport on many ministers owned a slave or two. The list included Joseph Moss of Derby, John Southmayd and Mark Leavenworth of Waterbury, Jared Eliot of Killingworth, Samuel Whittlesey of Wallingford, Daniel Wadsworth of Hartford and Nicholas Street of East Haven. Joseph Noyes of New Haven

RAN-AWAY from his Matter John Perkins, of Norwich, on the 27th of Auguft Inft a Negro Man Servant named Nero, about 20 Years old ; a well looking Fellow, of middling Stature ; had a fmall Scar over one Eye, and fome Scars on the back of one Hand ; fpeaks broken Englifh ; had on when he went away a tow Shirt and ozenbrigs Trowfers, grey yarn Hofe, brafs Buckles in his fhoes, an old grey ratteen Coat double-breafted, and no Hat ; he went away in Irons which tis likely he has got off. Whoever fhall take up faid Negro and convey him to his faid Mafter, fhall have Five Dollars Reward, and all necefiary Charges paid by me   JOHN PERKINS.

N. B. All Mafters of Veffels and others are hereby cautioned againft harbouring or carrying off faid Negro, as they would avoid the penalty of the Law.

Advertisement from *The New-London Summary* (1759).

bequeathed an estate of £3,600 mostly in land, four negro slaves and £25 of books. His widow manumitted the slaves. It was commonly asserted that ministers' slaves were noted for piety, gained presumably by close contact with their masters. For the ministers it was a convenient arrangement through which they had the work done on their farms.

The absence of *any* legislation concerning slaves from 1730 to 1774, when import of "any indian, negro or molatto slave" into Connecticut was prohibited, suggests a stable situation and no strong movement for abolition. Very few Connecticut citizens appear to have openly opposed slavery. Aaron Cleveland (1744-1815), minister for many years in Norwich and later elsewhere, may have been the first Connecticut writer to denounce slavery. On the eve of the Revolution he supposedly contributed the articles appearing in the *Norwich Packet* on the subject, and in 1775 he published an antislavery poem. Only after the war did the legislature provide for gradual emancipation, and not until 1848 was slavery finally formally abolished.

Slavery in New England operated with certain ameliorative conditions. In many cases Puritan masters wanted their slaves to read and write so they could perform work requiring these skills. If the various laws regulating Negroes comprised a sort of code, there is no evidence of rigorous enforcement. Also, marriage was encouraged for Negroes and the usual procedures, including publishing the banns, were followed. While no consistent widespread effort to convert Negroes to Puritanism was made, there was no prohibition against it and some were converted.

In summary, the Negro's status in Connecticut usually was one of slavery—but far less rigorous in practice than in the South or the West Indies. While Puritan slaveholders seem to have felt few pangs of conscience over owning slaves, they were careful to keep the number relatively small and thus avoided the nightmarish fears of insurrection which haunted other sections.

A Continuing Concern for Education

Throughout the colonial period Connecticut evidenced a commitment to education. The Code of 1650 required every town with fifty or more families to hire a teacher of reading and writing. When

A In ADAM's Fall,
We finned all.

B Heaven to find,
The BIBLE mind.

C CHRIST crucify'd,
For Sinners dy'd.

D The Deluge drown'd
The Earth around.

E ELIJAH hid,
By Ravens fed.

F The Judgment made
Felix afraid.

G As runs the Glafs,
Our Life doth pafs

H My Book and Heart
Muft never part.

J Job feels the Rod,
Yet blefies GOD.

K Proud Korab's Troop
Was fwallow'd up.

L Lot fled to Zoar,
Saw fiery Shower
On Sodom pour.

M Mofes was he
Who Ifrael's Hoft
Led thro' the Sea.

The New England Primer, a book studied by generations of children.

a town reached 100 families, it had to establish a grammar school to prepare youths for college. An ambitious youth thus could proceed through local dame schools which provided the rudiments; the grammar school; and, finally, to Harvard, or later Connecticut's Collegiate School—Yale. Very few made it all the way, and few even finished the grammar school.

The grammar school at New Haven founded under the bequest of Edward Hopkins seems to have been especially influential. Hopkins also provided a similar bequest to Hartford and it resulted in what was termed variously a "Grammar School," "Latin School" or "Free School."

In 1678 the legislature ordered every town of thirty (instead of fifty) families to provide a school to teach reading and writing. Despite such laws, the preamble to a 1690 law declared that there were still "many persons unable to read the English tongue." Moved by this unhappy situation the assembly ordered "free schooles" to be opened at Hartford and New Haven to instruct in reading, writing, arithmetic, Latin and Greek. At the same time the assembly required the towns to maintain an elementary reading and writing school for six months yearly.

Later in 1700 the legislature required that grammar schools be operated at the four county seats—Hartford, New Haven, New London and Fairfield. All other towns of seventy or more families were to support a reading and writing school the full year; smaller towns, for six months yearly. The colony assumed responsibility for school support to the extent of 40 shillings per £1,000 of the polls and estates. If this amount proved inadequate, a town could obtain private gifts, levy a town tax or charge the parents as it deemed fit.

In October 1712 the assembly made the society or parish, rather than the town, the unit for schools. Five years later it imposed on the parish the familiar pattern of a year-round (eleven months) school for seventy or more families; a six-months school for smaller parishes.

The last major colonial change, introduced in 1733, employed income from sale of western Connecticut lands to supplement other school revenues. This act in its wording clearly implies that some towns were seriously deficient in their schools. Perhaps this land in-

103

come influenced the decision in 1753 to reduce colony support from 40 shillings per £1,000 of assessment to 10 shillings.

In the late colonial period a few private academies appeared in Connecticut. One of the most influential was founded at Lebanon in 1744 by Jonathan Trumbull and twelve other local citizens. They hired Nathan Tisdale, a Harvard graduate, as schoolmaster in 1749, and for almost forty years he ran the school with distinction. At the start Latin scholars paid thirty-five shillings per quarter; reading scholars, thirty shillings. Trumbull sent his sons and daughters there, and the school attracted students even from the southern colonies and the West Indies.

The Reverend Eleazar Wheelock launched Connecticut's most unusual colonial school—one for training Indians as missionaries and teachers. In December 1743 a Mohegan named Samson Occum, recently converted in the Great Awakening, applied to Wheelock for schooling and was accepted. Wheelock instructed Occum for three years after which he worked effectively as a preacher among his tribe. Impressed by Occum's success, Wheelock decided to establish a school for training Indians as missionaries to their race. In 1754 the school opened with two Delaware Indians. The next year Joshua Moor, of Mansfield, gave a house and two acres of land in Lebanon (now Columbia) for the school which became known as Moor's Indian Charity School.

By 1763 Wheelock was instructing more than twenty young Indians—mostly Delawares and Mohawks. That year he petitioned the assembly for assistance. Impressed by the attempt to "promote christian knowledge and civility of manners among the Indian natives," the legislators commended the project and ordered a public collection—an action repeated in 1766. No public funds were ever voted however—an economy which may have caused the school's departure. Occum went to England in 1766; created a sensation with his preaching and personality; and raised a substantial sum of money. In 1770 Wheelock decided to move the school to Hanover, New Hampshire.

It is difficult to judge how generously the colony and local governments supported education. One obtains a very definite impression that most adults were literate and that the colony genuinely believed in education.

104

Yale Becomes an Important College

As one considers the frequent largesse bestowed upon Yale College one realizes that a strong commitment to higher education existed. In the 1701 act of incorporation for the Collegiate School, the assembly agreed to pay £120 in "countrey pay" yearly for its support. Later it exempted students from taxes and militia service, publicly commended the enterprise and urged contributions by the public.

As the years passed the legislature continued annual contributions of varying amounts and on several occasions voted them the income from the duty on import of rum. Whenever the college badly needed extra money to balance its budget, the rector would ask for a special appropriation and usually obtained it.

Present-day college students frequently complain about the heavy pressures of their life, yet few willingly would return to the regime at colonial Yale. The undergraduate's day began at sunrise or at six A.M. from March 10 to September 10 with morning prayers which featured reading of the Holy Bible and commentary by the rector. Then came breakfast for about half an hour. Classes occupied the remainder of the morning except for a brief break for sizings (bread and beer). Dinner, the day's largest meal, followed at noon. Students enjoyed ninety minutes of free time after dinner before they resumed classes in the afternoon. Evening prayers filled the hour from four to five P.M. Sometimes faculty efforts were supplemented by "analysis" of scripture by an older student. After supper students were free until 9 P.M. when there was a compulsory study period lasting until lights out at 11 P.M. Probably many students doused their candles in sheer exhaustion well before that hour! Even the "free" time scarcely was free for recreation as students were required to read the Scriptures daily and engage in secret prayer.

Students generally studied three major subjects and, in addition, had weekly disputations plus occasional declamations. Freshmen concentrated on Greek and Hebrew grammar plus a review of Latin. Late in the year they started logic. They were expected to be able to translate Biblical selections from English into Greek. Sophomores emphasized logic but continued languages, too. Juniors studied physics (natural philosophy) chiefly, while seniors specialized in mathematics and metaphysics. Both juniors and seniors continued some language and logic work. The three upper classes underwent daily recitations translating the Old Testament from Hebrew into Greek, mornings; and the New Testament out of English or Latin into Greek, evenings. On Fridays and Saturdays all classes labored over ethics, oratory, rhetoric and theology. Saturday mornings were reserved for recitations from Hooker's favorite book, Ames' *Medulla Theologiae.* As the European Enlightenment's influence spread, some of the scientific theory of Isaac Newton was introduced to students in the 1720's and 1730's. Because of interest in the Newtonian system President Clap and a tutor constructed the first colonial orrery, a crude instrument showing planets and the orbits of comets.

The normal course required four years for the B.A., plus three years for an M.A. One could also obtain the Master's degree in three years without residence by presenting a lengthy essay somewhat like a modern thesis. Interestingly, a requirement for both degrees was freedom from "Grose immoralities and scandals."

Student disturbances occurred fairly often at Yale. In 1721 an outbreak began with a food strike which Rector Timothy Cutler subdued. Even worse misbehavior followed—stealing of hens, geese, turkeys, pigs and wood; breaking windows; card playing; "Unseasonable Nightwalking;" cursing and using all kinds of "Ill language." Strenuous efforts by the rector and trustees largely failed to identify the culprits, but one student was suspended. Another student, Timothy Mix, received a one-year suspension for striking several other students, running away from school and fighting with a citizen of New Haven. Twelve months later, wiser and repentant, Mix confessed his errors, was readmitted and later graduated.

Changing Intellectual Outlook

The European Enlightenment of the eighteenth century exerted a great influence on English America. Especially significant were the ideas of Isaac Newton who substituted a natural for a supernatural explanation of our world. John Locke in his popular writings made it appear possible for men, by using their natural faculties, to bring their institutions into close harmony with the universal

106

order. Through application of reason the Enlightenment preached that mankind could eventually become completely enlightened.

English America's intellectual leaders—men like Benjamin Franklin, James Logan, John Adams, John Winthrop of Harvard and Cadwallader Colden—warmly accepted the Enlightenment, but quickly reshaped it into an American Enlightenment adapted to the American environment. Many clergymen, even in Connecticut, accepted the Enlightenment and became far more open-minded in meeting new ideas and problems. Although an intellectual backwater in many ways, Connecticut could not escape this movement. Yale became increasingly receptive to it, and Connecticut's contacts with such intellectual centers as Boston, New York and Philadelphia deepened its impact. The ideas of English political dissenters such as John Trenchard and Thomas Gordon received wide approbation and helped provide the ideological base for growing resistance to Britain.

Care of Unfortunates

In common with other colonies Connecticut had not advanced very far in the care of society's unfortunates—the indigent, crippled, orphaned, mentally retarded and insane. While the number of such persons remained small, they still constituted a serious social problem. Given the Puritan proclivity to equate poverty with sin and to spend public funds meagerly for social welfare, the solution of such problems posed major difficulties.

The Code of 1650 dealt with only one class of unfortunates— the poor. It assigned to the General Court the task of deciding which town should support a poor person. In other words, poor relief was made a local responsibility—a principle retained throughout the colonial period. The towns, in turn, having limited financial resources, generally tried to force relatives to carry the load. If none was available, the town would be forced to pay for lodging and maintenance.

When the British government in 1680 sought information as to care of "poor, decayed and impotent persons," the official reply indicated that each town relieved its own poor and impotent. Few needed aid, the report added, because wages were high—and provisions cheap. As for beggars and vagabonds, the government did not tolerate them, but bound them out to service. It constituted what today we would call a hardnosed policy on welfare.

Not until 1699 did Connecticut officially face the problems of the mental retardates and insane. Presumably, relatives largely had cared for such cases and the 1699 law still required that solution when possible. If responsible relatives were unavailable, however, the authorities next could draw on the estate of the "ideot," "distracted" or "non compos mentis" person, as they described such individuals. Lacking family or estate support, the town was forced to pay the costs. Connecticut largely modeled its act on one passed in Massachusetts in 1696.

A few years later in 1715 the assembly interpreted the degree of relationship required for support of retardates to include parents, grandparents, children and grandchildren. It would be a rare retardate who would not have one or more relatives liable for support!

In 1719 the assembly more clearly defined the powers of selectmen in managing the affairs and estates of poor or idle persons. They were even authorized to bind them out for service. Any person who felt aggrieved by the selectmen's management could appeal to the county court for relief.

Sometimes unusually distressing cases came to the assembly's attention. In 1755 Phineas Cook, a mariner, took Robert Cromwell, a "poor, helpless, decrepid boy" apprenticed to him, and literally abandoned him in a "helpless and suffering condition" on a remote shore of Long Island. Somebody found the forsaken boy and brought him to Greenwich where he obtained support from local people. The outraged assembly ordered Cook to pay the colony for all charges already incurred, including prosecution costs, and post bond of £500 for paying future expenses.

Cook remained true to character by absconding, apparently without paying his debts or posting bond, and his arrest was ordered. Meanwhile the assembly validated reimbursement to several persons who had provided support for Cromwell. The entire case suggests that the colony lacked any real policy in such matters but, if pressed in a specific case, would demonstrate a sense of compassion.

References Consulted

Bernard Bailyn, *The Ideological Origins of the American Revolution* (Cambridge, Mass., 1967)

—— "Political Experience and Enlightenment Ideas in Eighteenth-Century America," *American Historical Review*, LXVII (January 1962)

Arthur W. Calhoun, *A Social History of the American Family* . . . (New York, 1945)

Frances M. Caulkins, *History of New London, Connecticut* . . . (New London, 1895)

—— *History of Norwich, Connecticut* . . . (Hartford, 1866)

John Demos, *A Little Commonwealth* (London, Oxford and New York, 1972)

Alice M. Earle, *Child Life in Colonial Days* (New York, 1899)

John Hope Franklin, *From Slavery to Freedom* (New York, 1967)

Philip J. Greven, Jr., *Four Generations, Population, Land, and Family in Colonial Andover, Massachusetts* (Ithaca and London, 1970)

David Hawke, *The Colonial Experience* (Indianapolis, New York and Kansas City, 1966)

Charles J. Hoadly, ed., *The Public Records of the Colony of Connecticut,* IV (Hartford, 1868)

Winthrop D. Jordan, *White over Black* (Chapel Hill, 1968)

Sarah K. Knight, *The Journal of Madam Knight* . . . (Boston, 1920)

Ellen D. Larned, *History of Windham County, Connecticut* (Worcester, 1874)

Edmund S. Morgan, *The Puritan Family* (New York, 1966)

Bernard C. Steiner, *History of Slavery in Connecticut* (Baltimore, 1893)

Richard Warch, "Yale College: 1701-1740" (Unpublished Ph.D. dissertation, Yale, 1968)

IX The Puritan Becomes a Yankee

The Structure of Politics—Town Offices

Under the 1662 charter the colony enjoyed a remarkable degree of self-government. On the surface Connecticut's political life in the early eighteenth century appeared stable, conservative and democratic.

At the town level the voters annually elected numerous officials, including selectmen, treasurer, moderator, clerk, constables, grand jurymen, surveyors, fence viewers, haywards, tithingmen, collectors of rates and leather sealers. In 1730 Hartford elected sixty-two persons to fifteen positions. The most important position was selectman (called townsman earlier). In the intervals between town meetings the selectmen exercised the legislative and executive powers for the town. Their actions could be appealed to and revoked by the town meeting, but this rarely happened. Among many duties the selectmen provided care for the poor, maimed, feeble-minded and insane. Broadly speaking, they supervised and protected the town's morals. They particularly watched heavy drinkers, suspicious strangers, idlers and the like. They insured that every child learn to read and write and study his catechism. As towns grew in size the moral surveillance declined, but executive duties tended to increase. In the eighteenth century the legislature passed many broad enabling acts under which selectmen assumed new powers.

The relative importance of some town positions was changing. The constable, once a powerful town official, declined considerably as he lost his earlier power to collect town and colony taxes, and saw much law enforcement pass to the county sheriff. On the other hand, the town clerk assumed greater influence as the years passed. No one could make everyday town business move more smoothly than an efficient town clerk. Likewise, as towns increased in population, the treasurer's position involved greater responsibilities.

In 1702 voting requirements for town or county elections mandated a man to be an admitted inhabitant of legal age, a householder, a man "of sober Conversation" and owner of a freehold estate rated at fifty shillings yearly. Such admitted inhabitants participated in town government and elected town officials.

Structure of Politics—Colony Level

The upper house, or council, of the assembly was a highly prestigious body, which had remarkable stability in its membership. Each fall the freemen voted for twenty persons in a nominating election for the council. Numerous people received votes but only the twenty highest, including usually the incumbent governor and deputy governor, stood for election the following spring. Granted that the current incumbents were better known and listed first in the spring election, the longevity of service and infrequency of defeat was remarkable.

A study was made of the fourteen men (governor, deputy governor and twelve assistants) who comprised the upper house in 1740 to determine how long each man served there. The shortest period was 3 years; the longest, 41 (Jonathan Trumbull, Sr.); the average, 27 years; and the median, 26. After only three years of service Hezekiah Huntington was defeated in 1743, apparently due to his New Light views. He succeeded, however, in winning election to the lower house in 1744. Generally it appears that once elected an assistant one could count on re-election until death or voluntary retirement.

The typical assistant, as Jackson Turner Main has indicated, came from a prominent family, often with large landholdings, and usually had attended Yale College. Frequently he entered law, but sometimes business. He started in politics at the town level, moved up through election by his town as deputy in the assembly's lower house, and became a justice of the peace. If he had not acquired a judgeship before election to the upper house, he always did so eventually. Generally he was a Congregationalist, and frequently held a high militia rank. In the 1740 upper house *six* of the twelve assistants were judges and *ten* held the rank of major or higher in the militia. While the Connecticut upper house members probably did not compare in wealth with those of some colonies, and great wealth was not a requirement, they lived in very comfortable, and occasionally wealthy, circumstances.

In the lower house the pattern of tenure involved a high turn-

111

The first statehouse in Hartford, built in 1719.

over. Taking the May 1740 session as a sample, of the 86 present only 30 (or 35 percent) attended the May session five years later. Two of the 1740 deputies had won election to the upper house. A study made by George Waller, a University of Connecticut history graduate student, revealed that during the decade of the 1740's the turnover of deputies averaged 41 percent *each* session—the same percentage as the 1760's. This turnover was somewhat less sweeping than appears at first glance since there was occasional repetition of the same surname in a particular town, which suggests that close kinship was involved.

To vote in colony elections for members of the General Assembly one must be a freeman. In 1702 the assembly established as requirements for freeman a forty-shillings-a-year freehold estate or forty-pound personal estate, and a certificate from local selectmen attesting "quiet and peaceable behaviour, and civil Conversation." A persistent troublemaker in a town probably could not secure the necessary certificate. As the final step, a candidate must swear to the freeman's oath before an assistant or justice of the peace. Apparently as the colony grew in size and population, the assembly found that it required too much time to screen and accept freemen candidates. Hence in 1729 it turned over to the town government the admission of new freemen.

How many men were freemen? In 1766 Ezra Stiles estimated that only *one-ninth* the population rated as freemen. It is impossible to substantiate this, but even complete adult male franchise, if one judges by the 1774 census, would have meant only about *one-fifth* of the population.

Charles S. Grant's excellent study of Kent indicates that in 1745 some 76 percent of adult men qualified for freemanship; and in 1751, 79 percent. For the same years those who actually became freemen were 50 and 51 percent respectively! In further analysis Grant found that those who could have been freemen but did not, tended to be apathetic about local affairs and/or lived far away from the meetinghouse. Kent, therefore, had only about one-half the adult males as freemen, and another quarter or more could easily have qualified if they really had desired to vote in the colony elections.

In town meeting elections for local offices Grant found that from the 1720's on practically all adult males were permitted to vote. Study revealed that the top town offices were held by a small group or clique of the wealthy. These men seem to have attained their offices through shrewdness, drive and unusual leadership qualities. The clique constituted a permanent elite who pre-empted the important offices and conditioned the town's inhabitants to think as they did. With absentee landowners playing only a minor roll, the residents reveled in the opportunity to buy and sell land in Kent prior to 1760. Economic opportunity kept most men optimistic about their future and disinclined to challenge the ruling clique. Only after 1770 did overcrowding reduce wealth and lead to widespread emigration.

Political Elites Control Major Towns

In a recent in-depth study of the political power structure of the towns of Hartford, Norwich and Fairfield in the 1700-84 period, Bruce Daniels has conclusively demonstrated that a small elite group ruled. Their leaders came from the wealthiest class, and most of the top ten leaders from each town were descended from an original proprietor. Through much of the period a few families

113

held an amazingly high proportion of major offices within the town or as town representatives in the assembly. Frequent intermarriage among prominent families further cemented their power. From 1700 to 1760 in Hartford the Pitkin family stood out; in Norwich, the Huntingtons and Tracys; and in Fairfield, the Burr family. The Huntingtons and Pitkins prospered as large landowners and leading merchants, while the Burrs became great landholders through astute speculation. Neither the Great Awakening nor the American Revolution displaced or democratized this limited leadership. Although voting rights were widespread, the voters continually chose leaders from a small elite. Certainly these three towns, geographically scattered, suggest a deferential society. Common men deferred to the elite and seemed contented with their leadership, or at least were disinclined to displace it.

Daniels did not find it impossible for new men to penetrate the elitist leadership, but it was difficult unless one was relatively wealthy. The best occupations from which to advance seemed to be law or trade.

Hartford, Norwich and Fairfield were all old, populous port towns. Certainly similar studies should be made of a sample of later, inland hill towns to ascertain whether the same elitist political pattern prevailed.

Growing Diversity in Religion

The solidarity of the church-state alliance, supposedly cemented forever in the Saybrook Platform, provoked immediate opposition. The shocking conversion of Rector Timothy Cutler of Yale to Anglicanism in 1722 signaled the beginning of a new period of decline in congregational ministerial ability and authority. Both from within and without the Established Church faced increasing challenge.

In the 1730's Roger Wolcott, later to be governor, wrote a long powerful treatise on church government which vigorously denounced Connecticut's semi-Presbyterian church government and the consequent increase in clerical power at the expense of the congregation. He charged that ministers completely dominated the consociations created by the Saybrook Platform. This treatise, though never published, very much worried the ministry. Ministers nearly everywhere found themselves increasingly embroiled

114

in multifarious controversies with members. In many cases bitter disputes erupted over the minister's salary, as numerous congregations failed to adjust salaries to the rapid rise in living costs. The duty of the minister to denounce offenders in church trials, also, often won him deep resentments.

The extraordinary economic expansion occurring in the early 1700's created many severe and prolonged controversies in public life which carried over into the churches. Differences over elections, lands and public issues in general produced factions which split churches as well. Repeatedly the minister was hopelessly caught in the middle of such disputes. Perhaps the most basic problem of all was a growing indifference to the church manifested in a widespread unconcern for the growth of vice and impiety.

Religious dissenters also slowly mounted a threat to the establishment. While a handful of Quakers alarmed Connecticut in the seventeenth century, it was not until 1731 in New Milford that nineteen people formally organized a Quaker meeting. The first indigenous dissenters were the Rogerenes—a small sect which gathered around John Rogers of New London in the 1670's. Persuaded by Seventh-day Baptists from Newport that the Bible did not ordain Sunday worship and infant baptism, the Rogerenes began disrupting Sunday Congregational services. The Rogerenes soon gained some converts and adopted pacifism and faith healing as tenets. More traditional Baptists first held meetings at Groton in 1705. In 1726 a congregation was organized in New London, and was followed later by ones in Saybrook, Lyme, Farmington and Wallingford.

Despite strong Puritan dislike and fear of the Anglican Church it was destined to make amazing progress in the early 1700's. It started in Connecticut through the work of missionaries of the Society for the Propagation of the Gospel in Foreign Parts. In 1706 the Reverend George Muirson, S.P.G. missionary at Rye, traveled from Greenwich to Stratford; and returned to Stratford in 1707 when he preached with much success. The first Anglican church in Connecticut was built in Stratford where the Reverend Samuel Johnson conducted the initial service on Christmas day, 1724. The next year some Anglicans in Fairfield constructed a church. Johnson notified the S.P.G. that many Anglicans had been imprisoned for not paying taxes to support the Congregational Church. By 1734 New London, Redding and Newtown also claimed Anglican churches. The colorful and determined John Beach forsook Congregationalism in 1732 and shortly thereafter headed the Anglican church in Newtown. Thus by the 1730's the Anglicans had won a small but solid foothold in southwestern Connecticut.

A Great Awakening Stirs Connecticut

What caused a deep religious awakening to hit Connecticut so powerfully around 1740? In large part this awakening constituted a response to the declining state of religion in Connecticut. This situation had developed from numerous causes: (1) substantial economic gains with attendant materialism; (2) loss of the religious zeal of the founders; (3) lowering of religious standards implicit in the Half-Way Covenant; (4) deadening of religious interest caused by the Saybrook Platform; (5) distractions arising from the series of intercolonial wars; (6) energies increasingly sapped by political conflicts at town and provincial levels; (7) increasing strife within religious societies; and (8) general social disorganization, especially in the area of most rapid growth, the east.

By the 1720's it was obvious that the Established Church, rent by internal problems and increasingly challenged by Anglicans and Baptists, had lost considerable prestige. In 1724 the Reverend Solomon Stoddard preached a sermon on *The Defects of Preachers* which squarely charged Congregational pastors with the spiritual indifference of their congregations. He claimed that many ministers lacked saving grace and could not preach. As a solution he advocated appealing to emotion in preaching. Some pastors found his words persuasive, while others strongly denounced him. Broadly speaking, the protagonists emphasized *piety* as against *order*.

Gradually New England found itself caught up in a religious revival known as the Great Awakening. After a limited series of revivals in 1721, a much larger one, originating at Northampton in 1735, spread into Connecticut. It received a powerful impetus in the fall of 1740 when the renowned English evangelist, George Whitefield, visited New England. An extremely powerful and fluent preacher, he attracted huge crowds at his Connecticut stops and helped spark the Awakening. When he stopped at Middletown on

116

very short notice in October 1740, a crowd of between 3,000 and 4,000 gathered to hear him. Farmer Nathan Cole and his wife of Kensington joined a great throng rushing frantically to hear Whitefield. Cole noted that every horse "seemed to go with all his might to carry his rider to hear the news from heaven for the saving of their Souls." Cole himself was awakened by Whitefield's message.

Many men bowed down by a deep sense of guilt found in Whitefield a new hope. Reborn converts were told that by admitting and repudiating their sins they were no longer damned. Whitefield and other Awakening preachers emphasized that no amount of conformity to the established order—Sabbath observance, praying or obedience to the regular clergy—could earn one salvation. Without true inward grace one could not be saved. The crushing burden of fear of losing salvation and guilt imposed by Puritan rule had been too great for many. In Whitefield's words and those of his followers they found release from the old hopelessness and tensions and a rebirth of joy and hope.

The preaching of Whitefield and other itinerants carried many ministers and would-be ministers or exhorters into the revival or New Light camp. The more conservative Old Lights opposed the revival because of its disorderliness and challenge to the establishment.

The Great Awakening peaked in 1741-42 with a feverish excitement. As might be expected, the Old Lights, representing the political and religious establishment, struck back hard. They were particularly upset by the preaching of James Davenport, a Yale graduate who left his Long Island church to travel through Connecticut as an itinerant preacher. Many liked him, and his appearance in Stonington produced mass hysteria. Joshua Hempsted characterized his services as "Scarcely worth the hearing" and "all Meer Confused medley." While the Awakening affected all of the colony it seemed to find particularly fertile ground in the east. Among the most prominent Connecticut ministers of the New Light outlook were Joseph Bellamy, Benjamin Pomeroy, Eleazar Wheelock and Jedidiah Mills. As Edwin Gaustad, specialist on the Awakening, has insisted, the new movement was "great and general," and without limits as to geography or social class.

The establishment, in solid control of the assembly as well as

117

First Church of Christ, Congregational, at Farmington (built 1771).

118

ministerial associations, reacted vigorously against the Awakening with new legislation in 1742. This law forbade even ordained ministers preaching outside their parish without invitation, restricted an association's power to license candidates to its own area and banned all unauthorized preaching by non-Connecticut residents on penalty of expulsion from Connecticut.

Furthermore, the assembly sought to make examples by arresting the two most feared itinerants—James Davenport and Benjamin Pomeroy. At Hartford a mob, apparently infuriated by the arrests, tried to free the prisoners. Authorities thought it necessary to employ forty militia as guards. While Pomeroy was freed, Davenport was found guilty as a mentally unbalanced person, marched between militia to the river and deported to Long Island!

While the Great Awakening quickly lost its peak enthusiasm of 1741-42, it produced some profound immediate and long-range results. It tended to occur in congregations where the minister already had been favorable to revivalism. In this case usually the New Lights triumphed, and sometimes a minority of conservatives then affiliated with the Anglican Church. In some cases, where the majority remained Old Light, a determined minority seceded and formed a Separate Church, as in Lyme, Mansfield, Middletown, New London and Norwich. Other minorities joined the Baptists. Certainly the Awakening wrought a strong spiritual quickening.

While deep schisms and violent conflicts marked the early stages, the intense persecution of the 1740's soon caused a swing toward more tolerance. The 1750 revision of laws dropped the anti-itineracy act, and in the 1750's the assembly exempted certain Separate societies from taxes imposed by the Established society. Eventually in 1770 the assembly exempted protestant dissenters attending their own church from penalties for nonattendance at the Established Church.

In the shifting uncertain standards of the 1750's the assembly found it necessary to enact a law aimed at preventing bribery and corruption in election of its members. The statute provided that any person offering or accepting a bribe or other reward be liable to a fine, while a member elected through bribery be ineligible to serve. The very existence of this law eloquently reflects the decline from early Puritan standards.

The law reflects, too, the sharper competition for political office. A Wallingford religious dispute in 1759 afforded New Lights a convenient issue to employ in trying to unseat Governor Fitch and seven conservative assistants. Ringleaders included Daniel Lyman, a New Light of New Haven, and William Williams of Lebanon, later a signer of the Declaration of Independence. A slate was prepared and advocates campaigned throughout the colony. Despite these vigorous efforts, Fitch and six of the seven assistants won re-election the following spring. Undiscouraged, the New Light group continued its efforts to oust Governor Fitch and other Old Lights. Though unsuccessful in the council, they rejoiced in a substantial increase in New Light deputies, especially from New London and Windham counties.

As a long-range result the Great Awakening reduced the church's power and enlarged that of individuals. Religious liberty was the accidental but great gainer. Gone was the authoritarian Puritan Church of the early generations which had provided almost unchallenged religious leadership, defined the bounds of social conduct and symbolized communal unity. In the Bible State church leaders had worked intimately with political leaders. By the 1760's the Established Church, although still attracting a majority, had been reduced to providing only religion. A steadily increasing number found their religious life in a minority church or belonged to no church. Congregational ministers no longer could order or threaten, but had to rely on persuasion.

Evasive Relations with the British Government

Through much of its colonial period Connecticut managed to escape close surveillance from London, perhaps in part because it was a small inconspicuous colony. After the great shock of Andros' unpopular rule, Connecticut leaders operated warily to avoid further grave threats. In the early 1700's there were several attempts to revoke the charter, but these became sidetracked in the maze of partisan politics in England. Connecticut leaders, above all, sought to maintain their charter unimpaired.

There was a fairly steady, though not heavy, flow of correspondence between London, especially the Board of Trade, and Connecticut, as the Connecticut archives reveal. It involved such topics as boundary disputes; pirates; rates for foreign coins; currency problems; periodic questionnaires about the colony, and its replies; occasional instructions to the governor and company; injunctions to obey and enforce trade acts, and cooperate with the Vice-Admiralty courts; and notices of major events involving Britain, such as deaths of monarchs and peace treaties. The correspondence reflects a constant but not intimate relationship.

Being a semi-independent *charter* colony gave Connecticut an important advantage over the typical *royal* colony, such as Massachusetts, New York and Virginia. In addition, Connecticut early resorted to the practice of hiring an agent to represent it in London. Fortunately in the period from 1693 to 1763 Connecticut had an able series of agents: Fitz-John Winthrop, Henry Ashurst, Jeremiah Dummer, Francis Wilks, Eliakim Palmer, Richard Partridge, Jared Ingersoll, Richard Jackson and Thomas Life. Dummer, for instance, strongly resisted attempts by London to force surrender of the charter. The assembly esteemed Jackson so highly that it voted him an expensive inscribed piece of silver in appreciation.

Most colonies were required automatically to submit all their laws to the King in council for confirmation, but Connecticut's charter did not require this. After the Board of Trade received authority in 1696 to examine colonial acts, it soon demanded a copy of Connecticut's laws. Only grudgingly and tardily did Connecticut respond.

Soon afterwards a major Connecticut act evoked strong English opposition. In October 1699 the assembly transformed into law the custom of earlier years on inheritances by ordering probate courts to distribute intestate property in this manner: one-third of personal estate to the wife, plus her dower right; the remainder equally to the children, except the eldest son received a double share.

This law's validity received a direct challenge in the celebrated case of *Winthrop v. Lechmere*. John Winthrop, a grandson of Governor John Winthrop, Jr., claiming the law unconstitutional, assumed the entire estate of his father who died intestate in 1717. He lost his case in Connecticut, but carried an appeal to London. As a result, in February 1727/28 the intestacy law was disallowed as contrary to British laws. If the decision had gone unchallenged, it would have plunged the legal and economic systems of Connecticut into chaos. The colonial agents fought vigorously. Francis Fane, legal adviser to the Board of Trade, prepared a lengthy report which recommended confirmation of all lands previously settled, but advised new restrictions. Parliament failed to take action so Connecticut's practices continued.

In 1732-41 Fane completed for the Board of Trade the only broad review ever made of Connecticut's laws. He found that 75 of 387 acts deserved disallowance, but only 7 clearly violated English law. Although he thought that Connecticut's civil and judicial authorities exercised too much unchecked power, Parliament took no action.

Connecticut gained power because of the preoccupation of Parliament and the King with many problems which seemed far more pressing than those of one small colony among many American colonies. The series of major European wars between 1689 and 1763 particularly engrossed London's thoughts and energies. In these wars Connecticut played a loyal and honorable role. In peacetime, however, Connecticut's leaders followed a deliberate defensive policy of remaining inconspicuous in imperial matters, but resisting any attempt to weaken its charter rights. When the calm was broken, a properly respectful letter from the governor and the efforts of an enterprising agent in London usually would pacify officialdom until some new crisis elsewhere again diverted attention away from Connecticut. The colony benefited from the conflict between Whigs and Tories on one hand, and Parliament and Crown, on the other.

In summary, Connecticut's relations with Britain as of 1763 were neither close nor highly cordial, but a basic feeling of loyalty to Crown persisted. Under the policies of "salutary neglect" toward the colonies, practiced by Britain from 1721 to 1763, Connecticut almost entirely governed itself. Little wonder that an anonymous writer described the charter colonies of Connecticut and Rhode Island as "Republicks under the Protection of Great Britain, rather than subject to it."

Connecticut shared in the pride engendered by the world-wide victories of Britain—ones to which it had made a substantial contribution. Unfortunately new centralizing policies for governing the vastly increased Empire would greatly exacerbate relations between Britain and America. It was predictable that these serious attempts by London to strengthen controls would precipitate strong American resistance. Such was the case in America and in Connecticut after passage of the Sugar Act in 1764 and the Stamp Act in 1765—a story pursued in the following volume.

Acute Economic Problems in the East

In the three decades after 1690 Connecticut enjoyed a population explosion during which twenty new towns were organized. From 1700 to 1730 population increased by 380 percent. In Litchfield County a surge of new settlers largely filled up the countryside.

The east, however, seemed to suffer most from the economic problems attendant upon unusually fast growth. Norwich typified this expansion when in 1756 it held first place in tax assessments; and second, in population. Encouraged by the large volume of business generated in the rapidly growing eastern towns, merchants desperately sought additional capital to expand their operations.

Two closely interwoven problems plagued the section—chronic shortage of hard money, and almost complete dependence on Boston and New York for most English imports. Typical cargoes shipped from Connecticut had to be used to pay for goods already purchased in those ports. How could eastern Connecticut break out of its economic bondage?

There was no easy or sure solution, but one group of businessmen thought they glimpsed a way out. They formed the New London Society United for Trade and Commerce—an organization designed to raise capital for direct transatlantic trade. This would eliminate the middlemen at Boston, Newport and New York, and their high charges. Impressed by this purpose, the assembly granted a charter in 1732. Within its first year the Society began issuing promissory notes to subscribers in return for mortgages—in the process becoming a land bank. Their notes circulated as money, and the funds acquired enabled the Society to build a ship and acquire a cargo.

Governor Joseph Talcott and many assemblymen expressed great concern over the issuance of the notes since the charter did not expressly authorize such action. In 1733 Society agents underwent an intensive questioning by the legislature which declared that their notes threatened to defraud "many honest people." As a result of the inquiry the assembly found the Society guilty of mismanagement and ordered its charter revoked.

Doubtless this peremptory action stemmed partly from the western mercantile interests who feared any great commercial expansion in the east, financed by cheap money. The quick demise of the New London company, however, accentuated the east's growing indebtedness. The assembly felt impelled in 1734 to authorize up to £15,000 in loans to assist the New London Society in repaying its creditors.

The tightness of hard money plagued Connecticut as it did most English mainland colonies to the end of the colonial period. For a brief period eastern Connecticut enjoyed a special advantage —cheap inflated Rhode Island currency circulated freely and was widely used in purchasing farm produce for shipping. Again western pressure was exerted to secure assembly action in 1752 prohibiting further use of Rhode Island bills as legal tender, unless earlier contracted for. Connecticut creditors generally welcomed Parliament's action in the Currency Act of 1751 outlawing land banks.

The Susquehannah Company Invades Pennsylvania

It is scarcely surprising that eastern interests, joined by some western friends, spearheaded a drive to establish Connecticut in northern Pennsylvania. Some ambitious citizens had noted that the clause in the 1662 charter setting Connecticut's western boundaries at the Pacific Ocean placed much of northern Pennsylvania within Connecticut. So in 1753 at Windham they organized the Susquehannah Company with the stated purposes of spreading Christianity and promoting their own "Temporal Interest" in that area. Afterward in 1754-55, under very dubious circumstances, a deed for land in the Susquehanna River area of Pennsylvania was secured from local Indians. Land speculators soon joined potential settlers in displaying enthusiasm for Susquehannah Company plans and eagerly purchased "rights" in the land. Prominent persons such as Eliphalet Dyer, Samuel Gray and Jedidiah Elderkin of Windham; Phineas Lyman of Suffield; John Franklin of Canaan; and George Wyllys of Hartford provided leadership, and the assembly gave encouragement.

124

Governor Roger Wolcott and his successor, Thomas Fitch, whose sons were deeply involved in the Company, gave noncommittal and evasive replies to the protests from Pennsylvania. In 1755 the Company, now numbering about 850 shareholders, petitioned the assembly to ask the Crown for a royal patent. This the assembly obligingly voted.

The progress of this company soon led to formation of a second group known as the Delaware Company. Under even more dubious auspices it secured from Indians a grant to land between the Delaware River and the Susquehannah purchase.

The outbreak of the French and Indian War slowed progress of these western land companies and not until 1760 was the first Connecticut settlement made by the Delaware Company at Coshecton, Pennsylvania. Formidable Indian opposition, added to that of Pennsylvania and Britain, delayed Susquehannah Company attempts at settlement for several years. In October 1763 an Indian attack wiped out a small Connecticut settlement—the first so-called Wyoming massacre.

The increasing difficulties of the Susquehannah Company with Indians, Pennsylvania and London encouraged its opponents within Connecticut. Jared Ingersoll severed relations and joined the opposition. Meanwhile Eliphalet Dyer, sent to England in 1763 to secure a charter for the Company, failed completely.

By 1763 the Susquehannah Company had won substantial support within Connecticut, especially in the east, and had secured a toe hold in Pennsylvania. In the process it had aroused formidable opposition among Indians; Sir William Johnson, the Crown's Indian agent; Pennsylvanians; and British officials. The further unfolding of this dramatic story is delineated in the succeeding volume.

A Land of Energetic Yankees

In the mid-eighteenth century did Connecticut remain "a land of steady habits?" If one judges by the writings of Richard Bushman and Oscar Zeichner, the answer is "No!" As we have seen, many unsteady habits had developed as serious disputes erupted over a variety of political, economic and religious issues. The Great Awakening, the rise of the Anglican Church, sectional conflict, currency woes and the Susquehannah problem all accelerated the breakdown of the old unity. Very rapid population growth and the series of intercolonial wars further hastened social disorganization and disunity. The old politico-religious establishment was badly shaken, though far from destroyed.

In a recent book, *Peaceable Kingdoms*, Michael Zuckerman has argued strongly that the condition of communal unity, so apparent in early Massachusetts, continued throughout most of the eighteenth century. This interesting thesis has been sharply challenged for Massachusetts, and needs careful study for Connecticut. William F. Willingham has found an emphasis on communal harmony and consensus in Windham from 1755 to 1786. While one cannot question communal unity as a prime Puritan goal, voluminous court records and General Assembly proceedings present clear evidence of an impressive amount of serious internal conflict in eighteenth-century Connecticut.

The situation went much deeper than a matter of specific issues rending the fabric of society. The individual had changed from Puritan to Yankee. No longer did he feel a deep subservience to the ruling class or live tormented by guilt feelings. An attitude of fervent individual independence displayed itself on all fronts and Britain eventually would experience its sting. Avarice, shrewdness, aggressiveness and strong self-interest all marked the open drive for economic gain. The seventeenth-century Connecticut Puritan sought better living standards, but apologized for it. His counterpart of 1763 considered wealth a positive good for individual and state. If he had twinges of Puritan conscience remaining, and some did, he expiated his doubts through increased philanthropy.

This epochal transformation into the Connecticut Yankee brought many positive values to counterbalance the negative ones already cited. A relatively unfettered man, the Yankee could employ his talents more positively and effectively. All of his major institutions—government, church, school, business, agriculture, family and others—now could operate more freely and be more responsive to individual and community needs and desires. This situation produced both more contention and more creativity. When troubles with the Mother Country deepened, the new Yankee would prove a formidable opponent.

By 1763 Connecticut in most respects already had come a vast distance from the small, primitive Bible State of the 1630's. It had become a part of the mainstream in the new, rational western world which was bursting with new energies and new visions. Connecticut's people stood poised for their advance into an exciting future.

References Consulted

Charles M. Andrews, *Connecticut and the British Government*, Connecticut Tercentenary Commission Publications, No. 1 (New Haven, 1933)

Eben E. Beardsley, *The History of the Episcopal Church in Connecticut* ... I (New York, 1865)

Julian P. Boyd, *The Susquehannah Company: Connecticut's Experiment in Expansion*, Connecticut Tercentenary Commission Publications, No. 34 (New Haven, 1935)

Richard L. Bushman, *From Puritan to Yankee* (Cambridge, 1967)

Bruce C. Daniels, "Large Town Power Structures in Eighteenth Century Connecticut: an Analysis of Political Leadership in Hartford, Norwich, and Fairfield" (Unpublished Ph.D. dissertation, University of Connecticut, 1970)

Edwin S. Gaustad, *The Great Awakening in New England* (New York, 1957)

C. C. Goen, *Revivalism and Separatism in New England, 1740-1800* (New Haven and London, 1962)

Charles S. Grant, *Democracy in the Connecticut Frontier Town of Kent* (New York, 1961)

M. Louise Greene, *The Development of Religious Liberty in Connecticut* (Boston and New York, 1905)

Jackson T. Main, *The Upper House in Revolutionary America, 1768-1788* (Madison, Milwaukee and London, 1967)

Benjamin Trumbull, *Complete History of Connecticut* . . . (New London, 1898)

Howard F. Vos, "The Great Awakening in Connecticut" (Unpublished Ph.D. dissertation, Northwestern University, 1967)

Oscar Zeichner, *Connecticut's Years of Controversy, 1750-1776* (Chapel Hill, 1949)

Michael Zuckerman, *Peaceable Kingdoms, New England Towns in the Eighteenth Century* (New York, 1970)

Documents

The spelling is modernized except in the second selection.

The famous Code of 1650 as approved by the legislature of the River Colony brought together in compact form a fairly comprehensive collection of the principal laws. It seems almost certain that Roger Ludlow, the colony's only lawyer, prepared this Code. It would be difficult to find a much better reflection of Connecticut's Puritan society and its outlook. From the nearly four-score sections of the Code a few have been selected for presentation under the original title.

BURGLARY AND THEFT

Forasmuch as many persons of late years have been and are apt to be injurious to the goods and lives of others . . . it is therefore ordered by this Court . . . that if any person shall commit burglary by breaking into any dwelling house or shall rob any person in the field or highways, such a person . . . shall for the first offense be branded on the forehead with the letter "B." If he shall offend . . . the second time, he shall be branded as before and also be severely whipped. If he shall fall [into the same offense] the third time, he shall be put to death as incorrigible. If any person shall commit [such burglary or] rob in the fields or house on the Lord's day, besides the former punishments he shall for the first offense have one of his ears cut off, and for the second offense . . . he shall lose his other ear . . . and if he fall into the same offense the third time, he shall be put to death. [*Public Records of the Colony of Connecticut*, I, 513-14]

GAMING

Upon complaint of great disorder by the use of the game called shuffleboard in houses of common entertainment, whereby much precious time is spent unfruitfully and much waste of wine and beer occasioned, it is therefore ordered and enacted . . . that no person shall henceforth use the said game of shuffleboard in any such house . . . upon pain for every keeper of such house to forfeit for every such offense twenty shillings, and for every person playing at the said game in such house to forfeit for every such offense five shillings. The like penalty shall be for playing in any place at any unlawful game. [p. 527]

MAGISTRATES

This Court being sensible of the great disorder growing in this Commonwealth through the contempts cast upon the Civil Authority, which [being] willing to prevent, do order and decree that whosoever shall henceforth openly or willingly defame any court of justice, or the sentences and proceedings of the same, or any of the magistrates or judges of any such court in respect of any act or sentence therein passed, and being thereof lawfully convicted in any General Court of magistrates shall be punished for the same by fine, imprisonment, disfranchisement or banishment as the quality and measure of the offense shall deserve. [pp. 539-40]

MARRIAGE

Forasmuch as many persons entangle themselves [by] rash and inconsiderate contracts for their future joining in marriage covenant to the great trouble and grief of themselves and their friends, for the preventing thereof it is ordered by the authority of this Court that whosoever intend to join themselves in marriage covenant shall cause their purpose of contract to be published in some public place and at some public meeting in the several towns where such persons dwell at the least eight days before they enter into such contract whereby they engage themselves each to the other, and that they shall forbear to join in marriage covenant at least eight days after the said contract.

And it is also ordered and declared that no person whatsoever, male or female, not being at his or her own disposal or that remaineth under the government of parents, masters, or guardians . . . shall either make or give entertainment to any motion or suit in way of marriage without the knowledge and consent of those they stand in such relation to, under the severe censure of the Court in case of delinquency [in] not attending this order; nor shall any third person or persons intermeddle . . . without the knowledge and consent of those under whose government they are, under the same penalty. [p. 540]

PROFANE SWEARING

It is ordered . . . that if any person . . . shall swear rashly and vainly either by the holy name of God, or any other oath, and shall sinfully and wickedly curse any, he shall forfeit . . . for every such . . . offense ten shillings. And it shall be in the power of any magistrate . . . to call such persons before him, and upon just proof to pass a sentence and levy the said penalty. . . . And if such person be not able or shall utterly refuse to pay the aforesaid fine, he shall be committed to the stocks, there to continue not exceeding three hours and not less than one hour. [p. 547]

SCHOOLS

It being one chief project of that old deluder Satan to keep men from the knowledge of the Scriptures . . . and that learning may not be buried in the grave of our forefathers in church and commonwealth, the Lord assisting our endeavors, it is therefore ordered . . . that every township within this jurisdiction after the Lord hath increased [it] to the number of fifty householders shall then forthwith appoint one within their town to teach all such children as shall resort to him to write and read. The [teacher's] wages shall be paid either by the parents or masters of such children or by the inhabitants in general. . . . And it is further ordered that where any town shall increase to the number of one hundred families or householders, [it] shall set up a grammar school, the masters thereof being able to instruct youths so far as they may be fitted for the university. And if any town neglect the performance hereof above one year, then every such town shall pay [a] fine of five pounds per annum to the nearest such school until [it performs] this order. [pp. 554-55]

Tombstone inscriptions reflect much about attitudes toward life and death. The very eminent usually rated a more elaborately carved stone with a longer inscription. These particular examples were copied originally from tombstones in Guilford, Madison, Milford

130

and New Haven and were printed in the *Papers Of The New Haven Colony Historical Society*, III, V and VI (New Haven, 1882, 1894, 1900).

In memory of
Mrs Eunice wife of
Capt William Davison
who departed this Life
May 15 1776. being 23
years & 10 days old.
See there, all pale and dead she lies
Forever flowing from my streaming eyes
Eunice is fled, the loveliest mind
Faith, sweetness, witt, together joined
Dwell faith & wit & sweetness there
O view the change and drop a tear.

Here lyes ye body of
Esther Farrand daught
of Mr Jonathan & Mrs
Abigail Farrand who
Died Decemr ye 15th 1757 aged 3 years
Beneath these clods my body lyes.
To cruel death a sacrifice
No age nor sex from death is free
O think of death then think of me.

HERE LYETH INTERRED THE
BODY OF COLL. ROBERT
TREAT ESR WHO FAITHFULLY
SERUD THIS COLONY IN THE
POST OF GOVERNOVR AND
DEPUTY GOVERNOVR NEAR
YE SPACE OF THIRTY YEARS
AND ATT YE AGE OF FOVR
SCORE AND EIGHT YEARS
EXCHANGED THIS LIFE
FOR A BETTER JULY 12
ANNO DOM: 1710.

Jonathan Son of
Mr Jonathan &
Mrs Lydia
Fowler
Died Novm 1. 1794
Aged 7 Days.
An Early branch
A morning flower
Cut down and
Withered in an hour

In Memory of Mrs
Deborah Relict of
Mr Ebenezer Hall
who died October
27th 1758 In her 83d yr.
Behold & see as you pass by
As you are now so once was I
As I am now so must you be
Prepare for Death & follow me.

Ichabod Scranton
Father of Abraham Scranton
Was born Feb. 19 1717
He obtained a Captain's
Commission from King
George the 2nd and went
Into Canada during the
French War and Served
2 years returing home
Took the small pox at
Albany and died and was
Buried in Guilford
Dec 1760.

For the more distinguished sometimes a large, flat, table monument was provided. This is an example.

In MEMORY of
The Reverend and venerable
JONATHAN TODD, A M.
who was born at New Haven, March 20th 1713;
ordained pastor of the Church at
East Guilford Oct. 24th 1733;
and continued there in the ministry until his death.
He had a contemplative mind; read and thought much
was candid in his enquiries;
and in science, theology and history,
had a clear discernment and sound Judgment.
Singularly mild and amiable in his disposition;
clothed with humility and plainness;
Serene in all occurrences of life; a friend and patriot;
a most laborious and faithful minister,
guided by the sacred oracles:
eminent piety and resignation;
adorning Religeon which brings
Glory to God and salvation to men.
He died in faith Feby 24th 1791.
By his side lies interred his virtuous Consort,
Mrs. ELIZABETH TODD,
who died Decr 14th 1783. Æt. 73.

Joshua Hempsted (1678-1758) of New London wrote what was probably the most significant diary kept in colonial Connecticut. He enjoyed a remarkably varied career as farmer, surveyor, attorney, justice of the peace, judge of probate, house and ship carpenter, stonecutter, sailor, merchant, representative for New London in the General Assembly, executor of wills, overseer to widows, guardian to orphans, and militia officer. In his diary covering the years from 1711 to 1758 he recounted faithfully both the joys and the vicissitudes of everyday life.

133

Oct. 5, 1711 Fair. I gathered corn in Smith's lot and we husked the corn that grew in my lot at night. A very windy day and late in the night it rained a little.

Oct. 7, 1711 Mr. White preached in the forenoon and Mr. Hunting in the afternoon. The sad news came of a great fire in Boston. Burned from the Schoolhouse Lane to almost the head of the town dock both sides of the street. About 100 houses burnt and 8 or 9 persons lost.

Oct. 8, 1711 Fair. I killed a lamb in the morning and then about ten I went to work at the ship.

Sept. 25, 1712 I was on the grand jury all day. We indicted Daniel Guard for murder and Joseph Elderkin for counterfeiting a 20 shilling bill, that is, altering from a 2 shilling 6 pence bill to 20 shillings. He is fined £45 and a 6 months' imprisonment. We acquitted Wentworth and Hambleton for the same fact, and we acquitted old John Guard who was committed for murdering Will Whitear with his son Daniel, but only his son indicted.

Nov. 12, 1712 I was all day at the Court of Probate about Ebe[nezer] Hubbell's business. The Court ordered a distribution of Hubbell's estate to be made by Mr. Latimore, Mr. Green and Samuel Fosdick. Daniel Guard had his sentence which was to sit on the gallows with a halter about his neck and to be whipped 39 lashes and to stand committed till he pays the charge of his prosecution.

Nov. 21, 1712 In the forenoon I went to look [for] my horse and found him at S. Harris's. In the afternoon I went to see Daniel Guard remove his punishment. He was first to sit on the gallows 1 hour and then was whipped 39 lashes with a single codline at the signpost.

Sept. 25, 1713 Fair, cloudy. I was in town in the forenoon to see a man branded on the forehead for breaking open a house in Lebanon and stealing sundries, etc. I sent to William Starke by Moses Fish 29 shillings in bills. In the forenoon in town and in the afternoon gathering corn in Smith's lot and finished and got it in. Lydia Starr had fits.

134

Sept. 27, 1713 Misty. Mr. Adams absent. The Governor prayed and Mr. Denison did read and Robert, free Negro, and Hager, molatto, published [intent to marry].

May 23, 1721 Fair. I hired of Capt. James Babcock 114 sheep (their fleece on) and 108 lambs. I am to have them 5 year[s] and to give one shilling per annum rent and to pay annually on the 10th of June and to return them in the like good order as I received them. [There are] but 5 or 6 that are very old and 6 or 7 [have] very coarse wool. The rest likely sheep and well wooled.

Aug. 17, 1721 Some showers. I set out for Hartford. I got to Colchester about 9 o'clock. Lodged at Chamberlins. Expenses 1s.5d. not paid for want of change.

Aug. 18, 1721 Cloudy and showery. I got to Capt. Wells's to dinner. Expenses 9d and 2s. for tooth powder which I borrowed of Mrs. Wells for want of change. I could not get over for the flood. . . .

Aug. 19, 1721 Some showers. I got over to Rocky Hill for 2s.0d. and so to Hartford. Put out my mare to Barnerd's and lodged at Will Cadwell's. Stayed there till Monday.

Aug. 20, 1721 Fair and came away to Wethersfield and received my money for the wool £260¼ [and] about £17 15s. 0d. and £4 for pork.

Nov. 8, 1721 Fair. A Thanksgiving. Mr. Adams preached. James Beebe and Jane Plumbley published [intent to marry].

Nov. 9, 1721 Fair. I was at home most of the day. Toward night I went and pinned down some plank in Mr. Winthrop's bridge about 2 or 3 hours. Henry Joans [had] a child buried. Barnabas Tuthill sailed for Jamaica.

Nov. 12, 1721 Fair, cold. A sacramental day. Mr. Adams preached all day. John Moor, a daughter baptized Martha.

Nov. 13, 1721 Fair. A training day. The first and second Company in arms. I treated the Company with about 5 quarts of rum, etc.

Oct. 16, 1727 Fair. I set out for New Haven to the General Assembly in company with Judge Christophers and the sheriff and his man. We lodged at Buel's at Killingworth.

Oct. 17, 1727 Fair. We got to New Haven before night. I went to Mr. Gaskell's and we sent our horses to pasture.

Oct. 18, 1727 Fair, cold, windy. John Tongue's son George died. I went to the House of Deputies and entered and after a while the whole house waited on his Honor the Governor and the Deputy Governor and Council, and a great number of the clergy to proclaim the King George the Second. A great number of spectators. The troop and eight foot companies in arms—6 of New Haven and 2 from Milford. Major Eells disciplined the regiment. The sheriff on horseback made proclamation. Spoke every sentence after the secretary. Being done the whole concourse gave 3 huzzas and each company gave 3 distinct volleys and then 3 great guns were discharged. An ox was meanwhile roasted whole by the commission[ed] officers, which was distributed to the soldiers and a pipe of wine at the country charge and at night the courthouse, college, and several other houses besides the Rector's were illuminated. Bonfires and other signals of joy most of the night.

June 21, 1743 Cloudy. A small shower in the morning. Afterward fair. We began to mow. I was at court all day. Nathaniel Richards of Norwich, aged 50, was whipped 25 stripes and branded on the forehead with A on a hot iron and a halter put about his neck. Sarah Leffingwell, aged 50, had the same punishment except [she had] but 23 stripes. [*Diary of Joshua Hempstead* (New London, 1901), pp. 2-411, *passim*]

Index

Abercromby, James, 79
Abolition of slavery, 101
Academies, private, 104
Acadia, 73, 75, 76
Acadians, in Connecticut, 77-78
Adams, John, 107
Admitted inhabitant, eighteenth century, 110-11; under Fundamental Orders, 36
Adultery, 95
Africa, 89, 98
Agawams, Indian tribe, 22
Agents, for Connecticut in England, 74, 121
Agriculture, description, 81-84; dominates, 91; products, 87; reform, 84; use of Negroes in, 99
Aix-la-Chapelle, Treaty of, 77
Albany, New York, 74, 77
Albany Plan of Union, rejection of, 73, 77
Alexander, Sir William, Earl of Stirling, 43
Algonkins, confederation, 17; dialects, 17; dictionary, 65; religion, 19; tribes, 19-21
Allyn, John, 70
American enlightenment, 107
American Revolution, 77, 114
Ames, William, 8, 10, 106
Amherst, Jeffrey, 78, 79
Amsterdam, Holland, 10, 38, 88
Andover, Massachusetts, 96
Andrews, Charles M., on Fundamental Orders, 37
Andros, Edmund, charter episode, 69; fall of, 70; mediation attempt, 61; Saybrook attack, 62, 68-69; unpopular rule, 120
Anglican Church. See Church of England
Anglicanism. See Church of England
Anglicans, 115-16. See also Church of England
Anglo-Dutch War, 45-46
Annapolis, Maryland, 90
Ansantawae, Paugusset chief, 41
Antigua, West Indies, 89
Anti-slavery, Aaron Cleveland's role, 101
Archaeology, sites, 17-18
Archbishop of Canterbury. See William Laud, John Whitgift

Arnold, Benedict, 87
Ashurst, Henry, 121
Asia, Indians from, 17
Aspinwall, Nathaniel, 83
Assembly. See General Assembly
Assistant, 51, 54, 111-12, 120
Atlantic Ocean, 1, 3, 55

Background, Dutch, 10, 38; English, 1-11, 38, 42, 49; Massachusetts, 1, 11-12, 26-27, 35, 39, 43
Balliol College, Oxford University, 35
Baltic Sea, trade in, 3
Baptists, 115, 116, 119
Barbados, West Indies, 89, 98
Barkhamsted, Connecticut, 22
Battle of Lake George, 78
Beach, John, 116
Bear Mountain, 14
Beckwith, Goody, 94
Bedford, New York, 62
Beef, staple, 82
Beggars, treatment of, 107-08
Bellamy, Joseph, 117
Bellomont, Earl of. See Richard Coote, Earl of Bellomont
Bering Straits, 17
Berlin, Connecticut, 21; Indians in, 22
Beseck Mountain, 14
Bethany, Connecticut, 40
"Bible State," 120, 127; New Haven as, 39-41
Bibliography, 12, 23, 48, 63, 72, 80, 91, 109, 127
Black, Robert C., 51
Blacks. See Negroes
Block, Adriaen, explores Connecticut River, 24; visits Podunks, 21
Block Island, New York, 27
Block Island Indians, 27
Bloomfield, Connecticut, Indians in, 22
Board of Trade, answers to queries from, 82, 87, 92, 98; boundary dispute, 61; calls Congress, 77; correspondence with, 120-21; reviews laws, 122. See also Lords of Trade
Bolton, Connecticut, 21
Boston, Massachusetts, 21, 24, 25, 27, 33, 39, 44, 46, 49, 57, 67, 70, 71, 84, 87, 88, 89, 90, 99, 107, 123
Boundary, defined, 13-14; map, 60;

under Charter of 1662, 55, 124; with
Massachusetts, 58-59; with New
York, 14, 55, 57, 61-62; with Rhode
Island, 54, 59, 61
Boys, family chores, 96
Braintree, England, 9
Braintree, Massachusetts, 49
Branford, Connecticut, 41, 43, 56, 57,
65, 85
Brentford, England, 43
Brereton, William, 53
Bridgeport, Connecticut, 22
British government, Susquehannah is-
sue, 125; relations with Connecticut,
120-23. See also England, Great Bri-
tain
Brockett, John, 40
Brooke, Robert, second Baron, 53
Brookfield, Massachusetts, 66
Brooklyn, Connecticut, 99
Brownists, as Puritan group, 5
Bulkeley, Gershom, 70
Bull, Thomas, 62, 69
Burglary, in Code of 1650, 128
Bury St. Edmunds, England, 49
Bushman, Richard, 125
Butcher, John, 59

Cabot, John, 2-3
Cambridge (Newtown), Massachu-
setts, 11
Cambridge County, England, 6
Cambridge University, England, 8
Canaan, Connecticut, 85, 124
Canada, 74, 75, 79
Canonchet, Narranganset chief, 66, 67
Canton, Connecticut, 22
Cape Breton Island, Nova Scotia, 76
Cape Cod, Massachusetts, 58
Capital, Hartford and New Haven, 58
Capitalism, rise in England, 3
Cartagena, Colombia, 76
Castle Island, Massachusetts, 71
Catholicism, 2
Census, of 1756, 92-93
Central valley. See Connecticut River
Valley
Champion and Hayley, 89
Champlain Valley, 79
Champlin, Christopher, 88
Charles I, King of England, 6, 9
Charles II, King of England, 52, 54,
56, 61, 62, 68
Charles River, Massachusetts, 58
Charter Oak episode, 70

Charter of 1662, boundaries under,
55, 58-59, 124; Charter Oak episode, 70; contents, 54-55; mission
of Winthrop, 52-54; self-government, 54-55, 110; threat to, 59, 61,
69-70, 71, 74, 120-21
Chelmsford, England, 9
Cheney, Benjamin, 85
Chesapeake Bay, 90
Cheshire, Connecticut, 40
Children, in colonial family, 93-97
Chocolate factory, 84
Chronology, of Connecticut history,
viii-ix
Church of England, clergy, 6; crea-
tion, 2, 5; Timothy Cutler, 114; doc-
trine, 40; fights Puritans, 6, 8-11,
38; Great Awakening, 116-19;
growth in Connecticut, 115-16, 125;
James II, 71; opposition to, 5-6, 115-
16; reform, 5-6, 9
Clap, Thomas, 106
Clarke, John, 54, 61
Clarke, Joseph, 61
Clergy, difficulties of, 114-15; marriage
ceremony, 94; own slaves, 97, 100-
01. See also John Davenport, leader-
ship, Puritans, religion, Saybrook
Platform, theocracy, Thomas Hooker
Cleveland, Aaron, 101
Clinton, Connecticut, 22
Clocks, making of, 84-85
Cloth, English industry, 3-4
Coastline, of Connecticut, 13
Code of 1650, 15, 65, 93-94, 97, 101,
107; selections from, 128-30
Coit, John, 85
Colchester, England, 4
Colden, Cadwallader, 107
Cole, Nathan, 117
Collegiate School. See Yale College
Colonization, Cabot's voyage, 2-3;
English, 2-3; rivalry in, 2
Columbia, Connecticut, 104
Communal unity, degree of, 125-26
Concord, Massachusetts, 67
Confederation. See New England Con-
federation
Congregational Church, attitude to-
ward marriage, 93-97; challenge by
dissenters, 114-15; clergy own
slaves, 97, 100-01; clergy's difficul-
ties, 114-15; English background,
5-6; franchise, 36; Great Awaken-
ing, 116-17, 119-20; Guilford, 42;

Hartford, 47; Hooker's influence, 46-47; missionaries, 65, 104; New Haven, 40-41; picture, 118; Saybrook Platform, 114, 116; theocracy, 40, 41, 42, 114; Wheelock's school, 104. *See also* John Davenport, Thomas Hooker, Puritans

Connecticut, origin of name, 19

Connecticut River, 1, 13, 14, 16, 21, 24, 26, 34, 58, 59, 62, 68, 69, 93

Connecticut River Valley, agriculture, 14, 81-82; exploration of, 24; lure of, 11, 12, 13; settlements in, 24-27; war erupts in, 66

Conservatism, 47

Constable, 110

Constantinople, Turkey, 49

Continent, of Europe, 2, 3, 4

Conversion, of Hooker, 8; Puritan experience, 5, 8

Cook, Phineas, 108

Coote, Richard, Earl of Bellomont, 61

Corn. *See* Maize

Coshecton, Pennsylvania, 125

Cotton, John, 11, 12, 38, 41, 42, 47

Council. *See* Upper house

Council for New England, 43

Court of High Commission, 10

Courts, New Haven, 43; under Charter of 1662, 54; under Fundamental Orders, 36

Covenant, church, at New Haven, 40

Cromwell, Oliver, 34, 52

Cromwell, Robert, 108

Crown Point, New York, 78

Cuckoos Farm, 9

Currency Act, 124

Cutler, Timothy, 106, 114

Daniels, Bruce, 113-14

Dates, in Connecticut history, viii-ix

Davenport, James, 117, 119

Davenport, John, 17, 42, 43, 47, 52, 55, 56, 97, 100; early career, 37-38; founds New Haven, 39-40; goes to Boston, 57; Indians respect, 40

Davis, John, 3

Deer, hunted by Indians, 18

Deerfield, Massachusetts, 66-67, 75

Defense, intercolonial, 44-46

Deferential society, 111-14

DeForest, John, 19

Delaware Bay, 62

Delaware Company, 125

Delaware River, 68

Delft, Holland, 10

Democracy, Thomas Hooker's views, 47

Denslow, Henry, 67

Denton, Richard, 43

Deputy, 54, 111-12, 120; under Fundamental Orders, 36

Derby, Connecticut, 100

Diary, of Joshua Hempsted, 130-33

Dissenters, religious, in Connecticut 115-16

Divorce, 94-95

Dixon, Jeremy, 40

Documents, Code of 1650, 128-30; Joshua Hempsted's diary, 133-36; tombstone inscriptions, 130-33

Domestic system, English, 4

Dominion of New England, Andros heads, 69-71; marriages performed, 94

Dongan, Thomas, 62

Dorchester, Massachusetts, 25-26

Downs, England, 11

Drake, Francis, 9

Drunkenness, act concerning, 64

Dublin, Ireland, 49

Dudley, Joseph, 75

Dummer, Jeremiah, 121

Dutch, exploration, 24; oppose Pequots, 27; relations with, 39, 44-46; settle Connecticut, 24; surrender, 56; threaten Holmes, 24-25

Dutcher, George M., 37

Dyer, Eliphalet, 100, 124, 125

Dykers, John, 88

Dykers, Michael, 88

East Granby, Connecticut, 22

East Hampton, Connecticut, 21

East Hartford, Connecticut, 84

East Haven, Connecticut, 85, 100

Eastern Connecticut, situation in, 123-25

Eastern highlands, 14, 83, 93

Eaton, Theophilus, founds New Haven, 38-40; named governor, 43; owned slaves, 97; wealth, 41

Ecology, 16

Economy, agriculture, 81-84, 91, 99; analysis, 81-85, 87-91; English, 3-4, 6; fishing, 15; hunting, 14-15; Indians, 17-18; manufacturing, 84-85; Milford, 42; New Haven, 41, 57; of East, 123-24; shipbuilding, 85, 87

Education, Code of 1650, 130; description, 101, 103-04; Indian, 104; legislation, 101, 103; private academies, 104; *The New England Primer*, 102; Yale, 105-06

Elderkin, Jedidiah, 124

Elderkin, Joshua, 88

Elections, General Assembly, 111-12, 120; William Leete, 58; New Haven, 40-41; town, 110-11, 113; under Charter, 54; under Fundamental Orders, 36; John Winthrop, Jr., 51

Eliot, Jared, 84, 100

Eliot, John, 9-10, 19, 65

Elitism, in government, 113-14

Elizabeth, ship, 77

Elizabeth I, Queen of England, 2, 5, 6, 8

Elizabethan Settlement, 5

Emancipation of slaves, 101

Emmanuel College, Cambridge University, 8, 39

Enclosures, English, 3-4

Endecott, John, 27-28

Enfield, Connecticut, 13, 22, 24, 59

England, 38, 49, 87, 95; background, 1-11, 42; capitalism, 3; colonization, 2-3; Connecticut agents in, 74, 121; economy, 3-4, 6; enclosures, 3-4; foreign trade, 3; Glorious Revolution, 71; mercantilism, 4; militia dispute, 74-75; mission of Samson Occum, 104; mission of Fitz-John Winthrop, 74; nationalism, 2; reformation, 2; religion, 2, 5-6; reviews Connecticut laws, 121-22; social classes, 3; Susquehannah Company, 125; threat to charter, 56, 59, 61, 69, 120; woolen industry, 4. *See also* British government, Church of England, Great Britain

English Channel, 2, 38

English cloth, exported, 4

Enlightenment, 106-07

Epidemic, 1647, kills Hooker, 46

Esher, England, 8-9

Essex, Connecticut, 85

Essex County, England, 4, 6

Established Church, Connecticut. *See* Clergy, Congregational Church, Puritans, religion

Established Church, England. *See* Church of England, Congregational Church, New Haven Colony, religion, River Colony

Ethnic groups. *See* Acadians, Negroes,

Indians

Europe, 2, 3, 4, 89, 122

Exploration, America, 3; Connecticut, 24

Fairfield, Connecticut, 13, 31-32, 85, 92, 94, 103, 113-14, 115

Fairfield County, Connecticut, 82

Falmouth, Maine, 90

Family, influence in politics, 113-14

Family life, described, 93-97; in Massachusetts, 96

Fane, Francis, 122

Farming, described, 81-84, 90; dominates, 91; reform, 84; use of Negroes, 99

Farmington, Connecticut, 22, 33, 92, 115, 118

Farmington River, Connecticut, 16

Fenwick, George, 34

Feudalism, declines, 3

Fiennes, John, First Viscount Say and Sele, 53

Fishing, Indians, 18; white, 13, 15, 91, 99

Fitch, Eleazer, 89

Fitch, James, 65, 68, 71

Fitch, Thomas, 82, 120, 125

Fletcher, Benjamin, 74-75

Forests, 14

Fort, Pequot, 30-31; Saybrook, 26, 28

Fort Duquesne, 79

Fort Frontenac, 79

Fort Necessity, 77

Fort Ticonderoga, 79

Fort William Henry, 78

France, 3, 71, 75

Franchise, electoral, eighteenth century, 110-13; Guilford, 42; New Haven Colony, 40-41; under Charter, 54; under Fundamental Orders, 36

Franklin, Benjamin, 77, 107

Franklin, John, 124

Freemen, eighteenth century, 111-13; under Charter, 54-56

French, attacks in, French and Indian War, 77-79; King George's War, 76-77; King William's War, 73-75; Queen Anne's War, 75-76

French and Indian War, 77-79, 125

Fresh River. *See* Connecticut River

Frobisher, Martin, 3

Frontenac, Louis de Buade, Comte de, 73

Fugill, Thomas, 40
Fulling mills, 84
Fundamental Orders, author, 35; described, 35-37; Hooker's role, 35, 47; interpretation, 37; origins, 35; John Winthrop, Jr., 51

Games, 97
Gaming, in Code of 1650, 128-29
Garbrand, Susannah, 8-9. *See also* Mrs. Thomas Hooker
Gardiner, David, 28
Gardiner, Lion, erects fort, 26-27; in Pequot War, 28-29
Gaustad, Edwin, 117
General Assembly, Acadian act, 77-78; adultery, 95; agents, 121; Albany Plan, 77; Andros' rule, 69-71; bribery act, 119; creates war council, 66; defies Fletcher, 74; divorce, 94-95; education, 101, 103-05; freemen acts, 112-13; French and Indian War, 77; Great Awakening, 117, 119-20; King Philip's War, 68; King William's War, 74; lower house, 54, 111-12, 120; Massachusetts boundary, 59; meets at Hartford and New Haven, 58; militia, 73; negotiates with New Haven, 55-57; New London Society, 123-24; peddlers, 88; probate law, 121; proceedings, 126; Queen Anne's War, 75; re-establishes Charter government, 71; Rhode Island boundary, 61; Rhode Island money, 88, 124; selectmen acts, 110; slavery acts, 98-99, 101; Susquehannah Company, 124-25; under Charter, 54; upper house, 54, 82, 111-12, 120; welfare acts, 107-08; Yale, 105. *See also* General Court, Connecticut
General Court, Connecticut, authorizes Tunxis survey, 33; care of poor, 107-08; creation, 35; Fundamental Orders, 36-37; Indian legislation, 64; land grants, 34; mediation, 45; Pequot War, 28-29, 31; William Pynchon, 32. *See also* General Assembly
General Court, Massachusetts, 11, 26-27, 35
General Court, New Haven. *See* New Haven Colony
Geography, 13-16
Geology, 15-16
Gilbert, Mathew, 40

Girls, family chores, 96
Glaciation, 15-16
Glassmaking, 51
Glastonbury, Connecticut, 21, 85
Glorious Revolution, 71
Gookin, Daniel, 19
Gordon, Thomas, 107
Government, Charter of 1662, 54-55; elitism, 113-14; Fundamental Orders, 35-37; structure, 110-14
Governors, election, 36, 54, 111; Theophilus Eaton, 38-40, 41, 43, 97; Thomas Fitch, 82, 120, 125; John Haynes, 11, 21, 31, 36, 46; Edward Hopkins, 21, 36, 97, 103; William Leete, 52-53, 55, 57-58, 81; Gurdon Saltonstall, 94; Joseph Talcott, 123; Robert Treat, 66, 69, 70, 71; Jonathan Trumbull, 89, 104, 111; under Charter, 54; under Fundamental Orders, 36; Fitz-John Winthrop, 74, 95, 121; John Winthrop, Jr., 26-27, 33-34, 49, 50, 51-58, 61, 67, 84, 85, 95; Roger Wolcott, 76, 77, 114, 118, 125; George Wyllys, 97, 124
Grammar school, Hopkins, 103; laws on, 103-04
Granby, Connecticut, 22, 59
Grant, Charles S., 113
Gray, Samuel, 124
Grazing, shift to, 82
Great Awakening, 114, 116-17, 119-20, 125
Great Barrington, Massachusetts, 68
Great Britain, 59, 73-79, 89, 107, 121, 122, 123, 125, 126
Greenwich, Connecticut, 22, 56, 108, 115
Grenada, West Indies, 89
Gristmill, 84
Groton, Connecticut, 92, 115
Groton, England, 49
Groton, Massachusetts, 67
Guadeloupe, West Indies, 89
Guildford, England, 42
Guilford, Connecticut, 13, 22, 41, 42, 56, 57, 85
Gulf of St. Lawrence, 76

Haddam, Connecticut, 21
Hadley, Massachusetts, 67
Half-Way Covenant, 116
Halifax, Nova Scotia, 90
Hammonassets, Indian tribe, 22
Hampshire County, Massachusetts, 75

Hanging Hills, Connecticut, 14
Hanover, New Hampshire, 104
Harland, Thomas, 85
Harmony, 125-26
Hartford, Connecticut, 13, 15, 16, 32, 44, 45, 46, 51, 69, 97, 100, 124; Block explores, 24; election of officers, 110; Fletcher visits, 74; Fundamental Orders, 35-36; grammar school, 103; Great Awakening, 119; Indians act, 21; joint capital, 58; migration to, 1; political power structure, 113-14; population, 92; settlement, 26; shipbuilding, 85; state house, 112; war quota, 28
Hartland, Connecticut, 22
Hartlib, Samuel, 52, 53
Harvard College, 103
Harwich, England, 4
Haynes, John, governor, 11, 31, 36; New England Confederation, 45, 46; plot against, 21
Health, epidemic, 46
Hector, ship, 39
Hempsted, Joshua, 85, 117; diary, 133-36
Henry VII, King of England, 2
Henry VIII, King of England, 2, 5
Hertfordshire, England, 39
Hingham, England, 4
Hispaniola, West Indies, 89
Hodson, John, 88
Holland, 3, 53; Puritans in, 6, 10, 38
Holmes, William, founds Windsor, 24
Hooker, Thomas, 21, 34, 37-38, 42, 67, 106; as author, 46, 93; at Chelmsford, 9; at Esher, 8-9; conversion, 8; dies, 46; early career, 6, 8-11; education, 8; evades police, 10-11; Fundamental Orders, 35; in Holland, 10; influence, 46-47; New England Confederation, 44, 46; picture, 7; rivalry with Cotton, 12; Saybrook Colony, 27; Springfield, 32; travels to Hartford, 16, 26
Hooker, Mrs. Thomas, carried to Hartford, 1; marries, 8-9. See also Susannah Garbrand
Hopkins, Edward, founds school, 103; governor, 36; owns slaves, 97; plot against, 21
Housatonic River, Connecticut, 93
House of Good Hope, 24, 45
Hubbard, William, 12
Hudson River, New York, 21, 62

Hunting, Indian, 18, 40; white, 14-15, 25
Huntington, Hezekiah, 111
Hutchinson, Anne, 39, 46, 47

Illinois, 73
Illustrations, x, 7, 20, 33, 50, 60, 83, 86, 100, 102, 112, 118
Immigration. *See* England, Massachusetts Bay
Indians, 24, 25, 26, 36, 125; Algonkin confederation, 17, 19; attack Simsbury, 67; attitudes toward, 64-65, 68; Block Island, 27; census, 92; Deerfield, 75; distribution, 16-17, 19-22; dwellings, 18-19; economy, 17-18; food, 17-18; hostility, 27-32; hunting, 18, 40; Iroquois, 22, 75, 77; King Philip's War, 65-68; languages, 17, 19, 65; map of tribes, 20; Miantonomo affair, 44-45; missionaries, 10, 65, 104; Mohegan alliance, 29; Narraganset alliance, 29-30; New England Confederation, 64; Pequot War, 27-32; population, 16-17, 92; religion, 19; school, 104; sell land, 39-41, 43; tribes, 17, 19-22; wars, 27-32, 65-68. *See also* Names of tribes
Industry. *See* Manufacturing
Ingersoll, Jared, 121, 125
Inner Temple, London, 35, 49
Intercolonial actions, 44-46, 77. *See also* New England Confederation
Intestacy law, 121-22
Ipswich, England, 4
Ipswich, Massachusetts, 49
Ireland, 82
Ironmaking, 49, 51, 85
Iroquois Confederacy, 22, 75, 77
Italian city states, 3

Jackson, Richard, 121
Jamaica, West Indies, 89
James, Duke of York, 56, 62, 68. *See also* James II, King of England
James I, King of England, 6
James II, King of England, 69, 71. *See also* James, Duke of York
Jenkins' Ear, War of, 76
Johnson, Samuel, 115
Johnson, William, 78, 125
Jones, Mary Jeanne Anderson, 37
Judges, 111
Judson, David, house, 83

Justice of the Peace, 111, 112

Kensington, Connecticut, 117
Kent, Connecticut, 22, 85, 113
Kent, England, 42
Kieft, Willem, 45
Kievit's Hoeck, settlement, 24
Killingworth, Connecticut, 84, 100
King George's War, 76-77
King of England, Charles I, 6, 9;
  Charles II, 52, 54, 56, 61, 62, 68;
  Henry VII, 2; Henry VIII, 2, 5;
  James I, 6; James II, 69, 71; Wil-
  liam III, 62, 71
King Philip, 65-67
King Philip's War, 66-68
King William's War, 73-75
Kitchin, Thomas, map, x
Knight, Sarah Kemble, 95, 99

Lake George, New York, 78
Lake Saltonstall, Connecticut, 16
Lakeville, Connecticut, 85
Lancaster, Massachusetts, 67
Land, 12, 96
Land of steady habits, 125-26
Land tenure, under Charter, 55
Lane and Booth, 88, 89
Larkum, Job, 95
Larkum, Mary, 95
Larned, Ellen, 99-100
La Rochelle, France, 49
Laud, William, Bishop of London, 9,
  10, 38; Archbishop of Canterbury,
  38
Lavenham, England, 4
Laws, Connecticut, review of, 121-22
Lawyers, 91, 114
Leadership, analysis, 113-14; John
  Davenport, 37-40; Theophilus Ea-
  ton, 38-40; Thomas Hooker, 9, 46-
  47; John Mason, 28-32; John Win-
  throp, Jr., 49, 51-55
Leavenworth, Mark, 100
Lebanon, Connecticut, 89, 92, 104,
  120
Leete, William, 52-53, 55, 57-58, 81
Leffingwell, Christopher, 84
Legislature. See General Assembly,
  General Court, Connecticut
Liberalism, Thomas Hooker reflects, 47
Life, Thomas, 121
Lime Rock, Connecticut, 85
Lincoln County, England, 6
Litchfield County, Connecticut, 82, 93,
123
Little Baddow, England, 9
Locke, John, 106
Logan, James, 107
London, England, 38, 52, 53, 54, 59,
  61, 69, 74, 77, 81, 82, 88, 98, 120,
  121, 122, 123, 125
Long Island, 43, 57, 108, 117, 119
Long Island Sound, 14, 16, 22, 27, 51,
  55, 57, 62, 93
Lords of Trade, 13, 74, 81, 98, 107.
  See also Board of Trade
Louisbourg, Nova Scotia, 76, 77, 78
Lower house, 54, 111-12, 120
Lucretia, ship, 88
Ludlow, Roger, confers on Pequots,
  31; Code of 1650, 128; Fundamen-
  tal Orders, 35; Massachusetts con-
  federation, 34; settles Dorchester,
  Massachusetts, 25
Lyman, Daniel, 120
Lyman, Phineas, 78-79, 124
Lyme, Connecticut, 92, 115, 119

Madison, Connecticut, 17, 22
Magistrates, in Code of 1650, 129;
  under Fundamental Orders, 36
Main, Jackson Turner, 111
Maine, 44, 73
Maize, 17-18, 81
Malbone, Godfrey, 99
Maldon, England, 4
Maltbie, William M., 37
Mamaroneck River, New York, 57
Manchester, Connecticut, 21
Manchester, Earl of. See Edward
  Montagu, second Earl of Manchester
Mansfield, Connecticut, 83, 104, 119
Manufacturing, 4, 6, 49, 51, 84-85
Map, Indian tribes, 20; Thomas Kit-
  chin, x
Marefield, England, 8
Maritime, 87-90, 123-24
Market Bosworth, England, 8
Marlborough, Massachusetts, 67
Marriage, 93-97, 101, 129
Martinique, West Indies, 88, 89
Mary I, Queen of England, 2, 5
Mary II, Queen of England, 71
Mason, John, 25, 28-32, 34, 52
Massachusetts, 31, 47, 49, 51, 56, 65,
  69, 71, 91, 98, 108, 121; author-
  izes Connecticut settlement, 26-27;
  boundary, 14, 55, 58-59; commun-
  al unity, 126; Endecott's expedition,

143

27-28; family, 96; grants land, 34; Thomas Hooker, 1, 10-12, 46; Indians, 21-22, 45; King George's War, 76-77; King Philip's War, 65-68; migration from, 1, 11-12, 25-26, 39, 43, 49; migration to, 10-11, 25, 38-39, 49; New England Confederation, 32, 34, 44-45; Queen Anne's War, 75-76; slavery in, 98; takes Springfield, 32

Massachusetts Bay Colony. See Massachusetts

Massachusetts General Court, 11-12, 26-27, 35

Massacoes, Indian tribe, 22

Massacre, Wethersfield, 28

Massasoit, Wampanoag chief, 65

Mather, Cotton, 8, 9, 42

Maverick, John, 25

Medford, Massachusetts, 67

Medicine, 19, 51, 91

Mediterranean Sea, 2-3

Menunketucks, Indian tribe, 22, 42. See also Guilford

Mercantilism, English, 4

Merchants, 78, 87-90, 123

Meriden, Connecticut, 14, 21, 40

Mexico, 3

Miantonomo, Narraganset chief, 29, 45

Middle Haddam, Connecticut, 85

Middlesex, England, 43

Middletown, Connecticut, 13, 14, 21, 85, 87, 92, 116, 119

Migration, from Connecticut, 57; from England, 6, 10-11, 25, 38-39, 49; from Massachusetts, 1, 11-12, 25-26, 39, 43, 49; from Plymouth, 12, 24

Mildmay, Walter, 8

Milford, Connecticut, 13, 17, 41-42, 56, 57

Milford, New Jersey. See Newark

Military service, 73. See also Militia

Militia, 41, 91, 105, 111, 119; French and Indian War, 78-79; King George's War, 76-77; King Philip's War, 66-68; King William's War, 73-75; oppose Andros, 62, 69; oppose New York, 74-75; Queen Anne's War, 75-76; Pequot War, 28-32; quota, 28, 64, 66, 75, 76, 78, 79

Mills, Jedidiah, 117

Ministers. See Clergy

Missionaries, 65, 104

Mix, Timothy, 106

Mohawks, Indian tribe, 22, 32, 104

Mohegans, Indian tribe, 17, 21, 29-30, 32, 45, 64, 65, 104

Molasses act, 89

Money, 75, 76, 79, 123, 124, 125. See also Paper money

Montagu, Edward, second Earl of Manchester, 53

Montcalm, Gozon de Saint Véran Louis Joseph, Marquis de, 78

Montreal, Canada, 79

Moor, Joshua, 104

Moor's Indian Charity School, 104

Morgan, Edmund S., 95

"Moses his judicials," New Haven code, 41

Moss, Joseph, 100

Mount Frissell, Connecticut, 14

Mount Higby, Connecticut, 14

Muirson, George, 115

Murrain, Mary, 94

Murrain, Patrick, 94

Mystic, Connecticut, 29-31

Mystic Harbor, Connecticut, 31

Mystic River, Connecticut, 21, 29

Nantasket, Massachusetts, 25

Nantucket, Massachusetts, 90

Narragansets, Indian tribe, 17, 28-32, 64, 66-67

Narragansett Bay, 29, 55, 61

Nash, Thomas, 84

Nationalism, English, 2

Naugatuck River, Connecticut, 93

Navigation Acts, 69

Negroes, 36, 92, 97-101

Nehantics, Indian tribe, 17, 21-22, 32, 64

New Amsterdam, New York, 53, 56

New Britain, Connecticut, 22

New Canaan, Connecticut, 22

New England, 4, 16, 26, 38, 52, 56, 68, 69, 70, 71, 77, 87, 89, 93, 94, 96, 97, 101, 116

New England Confederation, actions, 44-45, 64; beginnings, 32, 34, 43-46; Dutch relations, 45-46; King Philip's War, 66; Miantonomo affair, 45; New Haven's complaint, 55

New England Primer, 102

New Hampshire, 44, 61, 88, 104

New Haven, Connecticut, 22, 46, 53, 57, 83, 84, 87, 100, 106, 120; attracts Winthrop, 51; Farmington River, 16; harbor, 13; industry, 84-

85; nine squares, 40; population, 92; settlement, 37 41; schools, 103; shipbuilding, 85; slavery, 97. *See also* New Haven Colony

New Haven Bay, Connecticut, 39

New Haven Colony, absorbed into Connecticut, 55-58; adultery, 95; background, 37-40; Branford (Totoket), 41, 43, 56; charter mission, 52-53; franchise, 40-41; General Court, 43, 56, 57; geography, 13; Greenwich, 56; Guilford, 41, 42, 56; land purchase, 39-40; Milford, 41, 42, 56, 57; negotiations with, 55-56; New England Confederation, 44-45, 55; opposes River Colony, 55-58; organization, 40-43; seeks charter, 52; slavery, 97; Southold, 41, 43, 56; Stamford (Rippowams), 41, 43, 56; theocracy, 40-41; war quota, 64; wealth, 41; John Winthrop, Jr., 51. *See also* New Haven

New Haven County, Connecticut, 82

New Haven Green, Connecticut, 40

New Jersey, 57, 65

New Lights. *See* Great Awakening

New London, Connecticut, 94; absorbed by River Colony, 34-35; arrival of Acadians, 77-78; conference at, 61; founded, 34, 51; grants to John Winthrop, Jr., 51, 84; harbor, 13; industry, 85; King Philip's War, 66; religious sects, 115, 116, 119; school, 103; Nathaniel Shaw, Jr., 88; shipbuilding, 85; trade, 89-90, 123-24

New London County, Connecticut, 120

New London River. *See* Thames River

New London Society United for Trade and Commerce, 123-24

New-London Summary, advertisement, 100

New Milford, Connecticut, 22, 87, 115

New York, 71, 78, 82, 107, 121, 123; boundary, 14, 55, 57, 61-62; control of Connecticut militia, 74-75; Indians, 22; threat to Connecticut, 68-69, 74; trade, 84, 87-90

Newark, New Jersey, 57

Newfoundland, 73

"Newhavens Case Stated," 56

Newman, Robert, 40

Newport, Rhode Island, 87, 88, 90, 99, 115, 123

Newton, Isaac, 106

Newtown, Connecticut, 116

Newtown (Cambridge), Massachusetts, 11, 26

Niantics. *See* Nehantics

Nicholson, Francis, 75

Ninigret, Niantic leader, 64

Nipmucks, Indian tribe, 17, 21, 64, 67

Nonconformity, religious, 5-6, 115-16

Norfolk County, England, 4, 6

North Carolina, 90

Northampton, Massachusetts, 67, 116

Northampton County, England, 6

Northfield, Massachusetts, 67

Norwalk, Connecticut, 13

Norwich, Connecticut, 13, 65, 68, 71, 84, 93, 101; growth, 123; Negroes, 100, 101; politics, 113-14; population, 92, 93, 123; Separate church, 119; shipbuilding, 85

Norwich, England, 4

Norwich Packet, 101

Nova Scotia, 76, 77, 90

Noyes, Joseph, 100

Occum, Samson, 104

Occupations, agriculture, 81-84, 87, 91; fishing, 15, 91, 99; law, 91, 114; manufacturing, 4, 6, 49, 51, 84-85; medicine, 51, 91; merchants, 78, 87-90, 123; Negroes, 19, 99, 101; professional class, 91; shipbuilding, 13, 85, 87, 90, 99; trade, 87-90, 99, 114

Ockley, England, 42

Ohio River Valley, 77

Old Lights. *See* Great Awakening

Old Stone House, Guilford, 42

Oldham, John, 26, 27, 28

Onions, in Wethersfield, 82

Orange, Connecticut, 40

Orient, 3

Oswegatchie, New York, 79

Oswego, New York, 78

Oxford County, England, 6

Oxford University, 38, 42

Pacific Ocean (South Sea), 55, 124

Packwood, William, 88

Palmer, Eliakim, 121

Paper money, 76, 77, 79, 87-88, 123-24. *See also* Money

Papermaking, 84

Parents, control by, 93, 95-97

Paris (1763), Treaty of, 79

Parish. *See* Society

Parliament, 71, 79, 122, 124
Parmele, Ebenezer, 85
Partridge, Richard, 121
Patrick, Daniel, 31
Paugussetts, Indian tribe, 22, 41
Pawcatuck River, Rhode Island, 54, 61, 67
Peddlers, 88
Peekskill, New York, 62
Pennsylvania, 55, 124-25
Pequot. See New London
Pequot Colony. See New London
Pequot fort, 30
Pequot River. See Thames River
Pequot War, 27-32, 34, 39, 45
Pequots, Indian tribe, 24, 64; aggressive policies, 21-22, 27-28; dialect, 17; fight war, 28-32; location, 21, 22; sell land, 24; size, 17; slavery, 98
Perkins, John, 100
Peru, 3
Peter, Hugh, 10
Philadelphia, Pennsylvania, 88, 90, 107
Philip, King, 65-67
Physicians, 51, 91
Pierson, Abraham, 43, 57, 65
Pine Meadow, Connecticut. See Windsor Locks
Piscataqua, New Hampshire, 90
Pitkin, Joseph, 89
Pitkin, William, 77
Pitt, William, 78, 79
Plains of Abraham, Canada, 79
Plymouth, England, 25
Plymouth, Massachusetts, 21, 53; Andros regime, 71; King Philip's War, 65-68; marriage, 96; migration from, 12, 24; migration to, 6; New England Confederation, 44; settles Windsor, 24-26
Pocumtucks, Indian tribe, 64, 66, 67
Podunks, Indian tribe, 21
Political philosophy, Thomas Hooker, 46-47
Politics, 35-37, 43, 110-14. See also General Assembly; General Court, Connecticut; New Haven Colony; River Colony
Pomeroy, Benjamin, 117, 119
Pomfret, Connecticut, 99
Ponderson, John, 40
Poor, care of, 107-08
Population, 16-17, 73, 92-93, 123
Poquonocks, Indian tribe, 22

Pork, 82
Port Royal, Canada, 75
Portland, Maine, 90
Portsmouth, New Hampshire, 90
Portugal, 3
Poverty, 107-08
Powwow, 19
Presbyterians, 5
Privy Council, 61
Probate court, 121
Profanity, in Code of 1650, 130
Professions, 91
Prospect, Connecticut, 40
Providence, Rhode Island, 51, 67, 90
Providence Island, West Indies, 98
Prudden, Peter, 39, 41-42
Puritans, 44, 49, 65, 107; attitudes toward family, 93-97; attitudes toward slavery, 101; change in eighteenth century, 126; English, 5-6, 8, 9, 10, 52; Fundamental Orders, 36-37; Hooker's influence, 46-47; in Holland, 6, 10, 38; in New Haven, 40, 42; migration of, 10-11, 38-39; persecution of, 6, 8-11, 38
Putnam, Connecticut, 21
Putnam, Israel, 79
Pynchon, William, 32
Pyquag, Connecticut, 21, 26. See Wethersfield

Quakers, 115
Quanehta-cut, Indian name, 19
Quebec, Canada, 75-76, 79
Queen Anne's War, 75-76
Queen of England, Elizabeth I, 2, 5, 6, 8; Mary I, 2, 5; Mary II, 71
Queen's College, Oxford, England, 99
Quenticutt, Indian name, 19
Quinetucquet, Indian name, 19
Quinipi. See Quinnipiacs
Quinnipiac. See New Haven
Quinnipiacs, Indian tribe, 17, 22

Radicalism, 47
Randolph, Edward, 69, 71
Rebecca, ship, 25
Redding, Connecticut, 116
References consulted, 12, 23, 48, 63, 72, 80, 91, 109, 127
Reformation, English, 2
Religion, before Great Awakening, 114-16; Great Awakening, 116-17, 119-20; Indians, 19; under Elizabeth I, 5; Yankee outlook, 126. See

also Church of England, Congregational Church, Indians, Puritans, reformation, religious liberty, theocracy
Religious liberty, 120
Retardates, 107, 108
Retardation, 108
Rhode Island, 14, 44, 54, 55, 59-61, 65, 66, 67, 88, 99, 122, 124
Rich, Sir Robert, second Earl of Warwick, 26, 49
Richardson, Alexander, 8
Richardson, Stephen, 61
Ridgefield, Connecticut, 22
Rippowams. *See* Stamford
River Colony, 40, 97, 128; becomes Connecticut Colony, 54-55; Dutch colony terminated, 46; founding, 2, 11-12, 24-26; Fundamental Orders, 35-37; geography, 13; Hooker's influence, 47; New England Confederation, 44-45; New Haven absorbed, 55-58; Pequot War, 27-32; Saybrook added, 33-34; Springfield lost, 32-33; John Winthrop, Jr., 51-55. *See also* Farmington, Hartford, New London, Saybrook, Wethersfield, Windsor
Rocky Hill, Connecticut, 85
Rogerenes, 115
Rogers, John, 115
Roman Catholic Church, 2
Rossiter, Edward, 25
Rotterdam, Holland, 10, 38
Roxbury, Connecticut, 85
Roxbury, Massachusetts, 65
Royal Society, 53
Rutland County, England, 6
Rye, New York, 62, 115
Ryswick, Treaty of, 75

Saffery, Solomon, 58
St. Eustatius, West Indies, 88, 89
St. George's Church, Esher, England, 8
St. Kitts, West Indies, 89
St. Mary's Church, Chelmsford, England, 9
St. Stephen's Church, London, England, 38
Salem, Massachusetts, 43, 90
Salisbury, Connecticut, 85
Saltonstall, Gurdon, 94
Sassacus, Pequot chief, 29-32
Saukiogs, Indian tribe, 21, 22, 45
Sawmills, 84
Say and Sele, Lord. *See* John Fiennes,

First Viscount Say and Sele
Saybrook, Connecticut, 22, 62, 69, 85, 94, 115. *See also* Saybrook Colony
Saybrook Colony, absorbed by River Colony, 33-34; besieged, 28; Captain Mason at, 29; settled, 26-27; Winthrop's desertion, 33, 49. *See also* Saybrook
Saybrook Platform, 114, 116
Scatacooks, Indian tribe, 22
Schenectady, New York, 74
Schools. *See* Academies, Code of 1650, education, grammar school, Harvard College, Yale College
Schooner, picture, 86
Science, 53, 106
Scotland, 6
Selectmen, 110, 112
Self-government, 54, 110, 122
Separate Church, 119
Separatists, 5
Sequassen, Saukiog chief, 21, 45
Sequin, Wangunk chief, 21
Settlement, Branford, 43; Dutch, 24; Farmington, 33; Hartford, 26; Milford, 41-42; New Haven Colony, 37-40; New London, 34-35, 51; Saybrook, 26-27; Southold, 43; Springfield, 32-33; Stamford, 43; Wethersfield, 26; Windsor, 24-26
Seventh-day Baptists, 115
Shaw, Nathaniel, Jr., 88, 89
Shaw, Nathaniel, Sr., 78
Sheriff, county, 110
Sherman, Roger, 87-88
Shipbuilding, 13, 85, 87, 90, 99
Ships, 13, 87, 90, 123
Shirley, William, 76
Silk industry, 83
Simsbury, Connecticut, 22, 67, 68
Siwanogs, Indian tribe, 22
Slaveholders, 97-101
Slavery, 92; abolition of, 101; beginnings, 97; election of king, 100; legislation, 98, 99, 101; nature of, 97-101; runaway advertised, 100
Social classes, English, 3
Social welfare, 107-08
Society, religious, 103
Society for the Propagation of the Gospel in Foreign Parts, 115
Somers, Connecticut, 21, 59
South Carolina, 90
South Sea. *See* Pacific Ocean

147

Southampton, Long Island, 43
Southmayd, John, 100
Southold, Connecticut, 41, 43, 56
Southwick, Massachusetts, 59
Spain, 3, 75, 76
Spanish Armada, 3
Springfield, Massachusetts, 32, 66, 67
Stafford, Connecticut, 21
Stamford, Connecticut, 13, 22, 41, 43, 56, 84
Stamp Act, 123
Stanley-Whitman House, picture, 33
Stanton, Thomas, 31, 65
Statehouse, Hartford, picture, 112
Stiles, Ezra, 83, 113
Stirling, Earl of. *See* William Alexander, Earl of Stirling
Stocking-weaving, 84
Stoddard, Solomon, 116
Stone, John, 27
Stone, Thomas, 1, 10-11, 29
Stonington, Connecticut, 61, 66, 92, 117
Stoughton, Israel, 31
Stratford, Connecticut, 13, 22, 83, 85, 92, 94, 115
Street, Nicholas, 55, 56, 100
Stuart, James. *See* James, Duke of York
Stuyvesant, Peter, 56
Suffield, Connecticut, 22, 59, 124
Suffolk County, England, 4, 6, 49
Sugar Act, 123
Surrey, England, 42
Survey of the Summe of Church-Discipline, 46
Susquehanna River, 124
Susquehannah Company, 124-25
Swaine, William, 43
Swansea, Massachusetts, 66

Taconic Mountains, 14
Talcott, John, 67
Talcott, Joseph, 123
Tariffville, Connecticut, 16
Taxes, 68, 79, 92, 103, 105, 110, 116, 119, 123
Thames River, Connecticut, 13, 34, 51, 93
Theft, in Code of 1650, 128
Theocracy, 47; Guilford, 42; Milford, 41-42; New Haven, 40-41; Stamford, 43
Thompson, Connecticut, 21
Tibbals, Thomas, 41

Tisdale, Nathan, 104
Tobacco, 82
Tombstone inscriptions, 130-33
Topography, 13-14
Tories, 71, 122
Totoket. *See* Branford
Town clerk, 110
Town officials, 110, 113
Town politics, 54, 101, 102-03, 110-14
Town population, 92-93, 123
Town tax assessments, 92
Toys, 97
Trade, 13, 99, 114; Boston, 87-90; coastal, 85, 87-90, 92; English, 3-4, 84, 89; local, 87; New London Society, 123-24; New York, 84, 87-90; Newport, 87, 88, 90; Nova Scotian, 90; Ohio River Valley, 77; slave, 97-99; West Indian, 82, 85, 88-89, 92, 97
Treasurer, town, 110
Treat, Robert, 66, 69, 70, 71
Treaty, Aix-la-Chapelle, 77; Paris (1763), 79; Ryswick, 75; Utrecht, 76
Trenchard, John, 107
Tribes, Indian, 19-22. *See also* Indians
Trinity College, Dublin, 49
Trumbull, Benjamin, 70
Trumbull, James Hammond, 17
Trumbull, Jonathan, Sr., 89, 104, 111
Trumbull, Joseph, 89, 90
Trumbull, Fitch and Trumbull, 89
Tunxis. *See* Farmington
Tunxis, Indian tribe, 22
Tunxis River, Connecticut, 33
Turks Island, West Indies, 89
Turner, Nathaniel, 41, 43

Uncas, Mohegan chief, 21, 29-30, 45, 64, 65, 66, 68
Underhill, John, 29-30
Union, Connecticut, 21
Upper house, 54, 82, 111-12, 120
Utrecht, Treaty of, 76

Vagabonds, treatment, 107-08
Van Curler, Jacob, 24
Vandervoort, Peter, 88
Vaughan, Alden, 65
Venice, Italy, 49
Vermont, 82
Vernon, Connecticut, 21
Virginia, 27, 82, 121
Voters, eighteenth century, 110-13;

Guilford, 42; New Haven, 40-41; River Colony, 35-36; under charter, 54; under Fundamental Orders, 36

Wade, Elizabeth, 94
Wade, Robert, 94
Wadsworth, Daniel, 100
Wadsworth, Joseph, 70, 74
Wahginnacut, Podunk chief, 21
Waller, George, 112
Wallingford, Connecticut, 40, 92, 100, 115, 120
Wampanoags, Indian tribe, 65, 66
Wangunks, Indian tribe, 21
Warehouse Point, Connecticut, 21
Warham, John, 25
Wars, Anglo-Dutch, 45-46; French and Indian, 77-79; Jenkins' Ear, 76; King George's, 76-77; King Philip's, 65-68; King William's, 73-75; Pequot, 27-32, 39; Queen Anne's, 75-76
Warwick, Earl of. See Sir Robert Rich, second Earl of Warwick
Warwick Patent, 26, 54
Washington, George, 77
Water, 13, 15
Waterbury, Connecticut, 22, 92, 100
Waterpower, 15
Waters, Josiah, 88
Watertown, Massachusetts, 26
Wealth, 41, 100-01, 111, 126
Weatogue, Connecticut, 22
Weavers, Flemish, 4
Welfare, 107-08
Wells, Thomas, 34
Wepowaug. See Milford
West Hartford, Connecticut, 21
West Indies, 82, 85, 87, 88-89, 97, 99, 101, 104
Westerly, Rhode Island, 61
Western highlands, 14, 83, 93
Wethersfield, Connecticut, 21, 41, 43, 82; Fundamental Orders, 35-36; massacre, 28; settlement, 26; shipbuilding, 85; war quota, 28
Weymouth, Massachusetts, 67
Wharton, Isaac, 88
Wharton, Thomas, 88
Wheelock, Eleazar, 104, 117
Whigs, 71, 122
Whitefield, George, 116-17
Whitfield, Henry, 42
Whitgift, John, Archbishop of Canterbury, 6

Whiting, William, 21, 53, 59, 75, 78
Whittlesey, Samuel, 100
Wickford, Rhode Island, 67
Wilks, Francis, 121
Will and Doom, 70
William III, King of England, 62, 71
Williams, Elisha, 77, 89
Williams, Roger, 11, 19, 28, 47, 51, 67
Williams, William, 120
Williams, Trumbull and Pitkin, 89
Willingham, William, 126
Wilton, Connecticut, 22
Windham, Connecticut, 88, 89, 100, 124, 126
Windham County, Connecticut, 99, 120
Windsor, Connecticut, 16; Fundamental Orders, 35-36; Indians, 22; population, 92; settlement, 24-26, 44; tobacco, 82; war quota, 28
Windsor Locks, Connecticut, 67
Winslow, Edward, 24
Winthrop, Fitz-John, 74, 95, 121
Winthrop, John, Jr., Charter mission, 52-54; children, 95; death, 58, 67; early career, 49, 51; elected governor, 51; Ipswich, 49; ironmaking, 85; negotiates with Dr. Clarke, 61; negotiates with New Haven, 55-57; New Haven resident, 51; New London resident, 51; physician, 51; picture, 50; Royal Society, 53; sawmill, 84; Saybrook, 26-27, 33-34
Winthrop, John, Sr., 39, 44, 45, 47, 49
Winthrop, John, grandson of John Winthrop, Jr., 121
Winthrop, John, Harvard professor, 107
Winthrop v. Lechmere, 121
Wolcott, Roger, 76, 77, 114, 125
Wolfe, James, 79
Women, age at marriage, 95-96; common law marriage, 94; denied vote, 36; divorce, 94-95; family life, 93-97; number of children, 96; status in marriage, 93
Woodbridge, Connecticut, 40
Woodbury, Connecticut, 93
Woodstock, Connecticut, 21, 59
Woodward, Nathaniel, 58
Woodward-Saffery line, 58
Woolen industry, English, 4, 6
Wopigwooit, Pequot chief, 27
Worsley, Benjamin, 53
Wyllys, George, 97, 124

Wyllys, Samuel, 70
Wyoming massacre, 125

Yale College, 59, 103, 107, 111, 114, 117; beginnings, 105-06; curriculum, 105-06; discipline, 106
Yankee, 125-26

York, Duke of. *See* James, Duke of York
Youngs, John, 43
Young(s), Seth, 85

Zeichner, Oscar, 125
Zuckerman, Michael, 126

DUE